THOUGHTRAVE

Before you start to read this book, take this moment to think about making a donation to punctum books, an independent non-profit press

@ https://punctumbooks.com/support

If you're reading the e-book, you can click on the image below to go directly to our donations site. Any amount, no matter the size, is appreciated and will help us to keep our ship of fools afloat. Contributions from dedicated readers will also help us to keep our commons open and to cultivate new work that can't find a welcoming port elsewhere. Our adventure is not possible without your support. Vive la open-access.

Fig. 1. Hieronymus Bosch, *Ship of Fools* (1490–1500)

First published in 2016 by punctum books, Earth, Milky Way.
www. punctumbooks.com

ISBN-13: 978-0692686911
ISBN-10: 0692686916

Library of Congress Cataloging Data is available from the Library of Congress

Cover image: Simrock × Vigiletti
Book design: Vincent W.J. van Gerven Oei
Proofreading: Michelle Baum, Andrew Doty, Natalia Tuero

thoughtRAVE

An Interdimensional Conversation with
Lady Gaga

by Robert Craig Baum

punctum books

CONTENTS

INTRODUCTION

IN HAND-TO-HAND BATTLE FOR THE USERS

by George Elerick

"Music is a moral law. It gives soul to the universe, wings to the mind, flight to the imagination, and charm and gaiety to life and to everything."

– Plato

In the movie *Being John Malkovich,* we enter into the mind of the title character, also played by John Malkovich. However, we experience not the view of John Malkovich but the subjective perspective of John Cusack's character, a puppeteer-turned-desk-clerk. The film is a form of transgression. It plays upon the desire to know (the impossibility of) what someone else is thinking and feeling, which is something we are told we can never know. The whole narrative violates and contravenes the social etiquette of personal privacy.

The book you hold in your hands easily falls into the category of a transgression. It's as though we are breaking into somewhere we are not meant to be (like a rave) and are invited into the mind of one of today's musical geniuses. Maybe we can even equivocate the experience to that of being a member of the paparazzi. Their whole mode of employment is based on breaking social codes and entering into the lives of everyday-people-turned-rock-stars.

That's what this book is, a disruptive invitation to break into the life and mind of Lady Gaga, the person, not just the persona. But, to understand Lady Gaga, we first have to understand the collaborative nature of music and the philosophical dialogue made famous by Plato.

Music exists not only for our direct pleasure; it also exists to inform us of the nature of reality, of ourselves, of one another. It has been part of the human story since the beginning. From palaeolithic tribes to the Pythagoreans who married music to mathematics and the universe. This marrying is the uniting of two seemingly opposite characteristics and putting them together as if they existed in harmony.

Much like marrying the night and day together. Or darkness and light. Or good and evil. This merging itself already seems to promote a new kind of transgression: one that challenges the systematic defense that all of the universe is separate and fragmented. That we simply accept scientific information as the reigning authority on how we live and experience existence. That we just take the fact that we all live on Planet Earth and that the sun is millions of miles away, rather than realizing that there is a relationship between the sun and the earth. The earth receives almost all of its energy from the sun. Without the gravity from the sun, the earth would not remain in orbit. So, two objects seemingly million miles apart work together in harmony.

Essentially, the spirit of music is to bring us all, seemingly different, together. The position of Lady Gaga's music is one that desires to unite our differences, to unite us all despite our worldviews, to celebrate one another. To celebrate the very things that distinguish one from the other. The venue to do this could be your bedroom, your iPod, a concert, or even a poorly lit dance floor.

❁

The friendship that developed between LG & RCB one would assume highly unlikely without social media. An international pop-star from New York City and philosopher from Long Island living in Vermont. This relationship is itself indicative of the nature of this very conversation, the hoped-for use of Google Hangouts and Facebook and Skype.

Thoughtrave breaks all the boundaries of expectation, language, and social convention. This on-the-go dialogue is not some pre-scripted interview on the nightly news or trending *TMZ* featurette. It's a conversation between two friends creating another dimension to their everyday lives inside social media.

You can imagine one of the scenes: after a busy few months of concert tours, Lady Gaga sits down to rest and take in the scenery she hasn't had a chance to truly experience for months, and out of her mouth, from the corners of her mind, emerges this poetic expulsion of angst, passion, and art all converging through the vehicle that is her music. Her body is simply possessed by something larger than her.

The role of music is not just as a form of feel-good entertainment, but something that invokes new forms of human subjectivity and experience. RCB & LG create a menagerie of views, perspectives, and methods on how to make sure that music elicits creators and not just passive, opiated, mindless consumers. This interview is more than a window into the mind of an artist; it is a confession to a friend, a confession to the world. This confession is not just from a human, but as if the confession is from music through the vehicle of the person of Lady Gaga: music as it transposes itself through time, space, and the multiverse.

To say music is transformative, however, would be extremely reductionistic and cliché. Music is not merely transformative; such a view assumes that reality is fine as it is. And as long as we change a few things around, reality could be utopia. No. It seems the goal of music is not to transform society; it is to simultaneously destroy the very fabric that holds it together and to give us the tools to build again. Music creates new realities; it doesn't transform old ones. I believe this transporting, transceiving function drives these friends to discuss in public some of the most difficult topics mass media has tackled as of late.

In an interview in 2013, Lady Gaga was asked about what her album *Artpop* hoped to do. Her response is one that should be listened to intently. "So the intention of the album was to put art culture into pop music, a reverse of Warhol," she explained. "Instead of putting pop onto the canvas, we wanted to put the art onto the soup can." This desire for art to pervade reality is something that is extremely powerful in the sense that if this intention were realized in society, class systems, art privatization, art patrons, and the whole commodification of the art object would then be turned in on itself.

A form of self-parody of an already-happened-inverse, Gaga (as commodity, as spectacle) deconstructs the very commodification of society and everyday life. So, this notion that art should and can belong to all isn't a new concept but is new to a Western society that praises the god of the commodity coupled with the illusion of individuality.

Although *Artpop* wasn't "well-received" by some critics, I think this rejection is itself telling of the culture within which it lives, not of the calibre of Lady Gaga's work. It would be too close to home for some. It would be like staring into a mirror and peering back are the monsters of privatization and individualism. Lady Gaga's fight should be our fight. A fight for freedom for all, not just for the few, a leveling of the horizon into a new horizon where equality is synonymous with what music as art can evoke.

So, is music meant to be just entertainment? Is this preface overstating its case? Is there more to music than meets the eye? What if there is? What if what we hear is not what we are actually hearing? These questions are the seedbed for the groundbreaking conversation through which you will journey.

To the reader: be open; be ready. It might change you – it might change everything you think you know. Turning on your radio is no longer something you just do to listen to music; now it takes on a symbolic role. You turn on the radio or press play on your mobile to be transported to another dimension. One where you exist between who you are and who you could be. Between how others see you and the very essence that ties your soul together.

PART I

#LG+RCB_
GO_HACKING

"Into these histories I commit myself
From these histories I am created
I am mother Monster
But you may call me Lady Gaga"

– Stefani Germanotta
(August 2013)

ON THE USERS

We meet in the middle of chaos, a difficult fall of 2013 for us both. For her, the difficulties of the Artpop launch; for me, the ongoing drama of entertainment production, higher education, and recovering from fifteen years of being an adjunct. Our exchanges intensify during the Polar Vortex of 2014.

ROBERT CRAIG BAUM: I've sensed you're "up to something" from the first time I put on the studio headphones to listen to the whole *Born This Way* album and then again with *Artpop*. But, I didn't fully realize this hidden world until I took the time to isolate... and really sit and listen... without satellite or FM frequency interference. So... Stefani...

LADY GAGA: Yes?

What are you up to? (lolol)

The music I create is an electric map[1] for the mind and psyche...

Okay. That was unexpected. Right from the top, huh? Going there already. Okay. This is such a beautiful image and kinetic description of what I personally experience as a listener.

Inside your brain there are pathways that electrical signals take... these are created over time by the things you watch, listen to, and what you were taught. Now we know that the way your brain has been trained to operate is incorrect – crisscrossed and cut wires and

---

[1] In a follow-up, we talked about the Sainte Chapelle rose window. LG responded that the rose window pattern is a very good way to describe how she visualizes herself in the "electric" auratic information received and transceived by her music, especially "Judas" and "Swine."

incorrect pathways that cause things like depression and anxiety and ultimately lead you to be unhappy. I use audio waves to cause certain pathways that have been broken or misused through the natural course of your lives in order to remap those pathways in a more correct and productive way. Audio causes neurons in your brain to activate the pathways they were designed to use.[2]

I wonder if this electricity creates different feedback loops for different people. Like how a fan reacts versus a critic's thousand word review. Then, consider a new listener or a whole industry of listeners with different, competing agendas.

I don't think about that. Ever. My music, like this discussion, is a remapping and reactivating of the electrical pathways in the theoretical mind of the human that the remote user operates.

Remote user?

The reason I may refer to a person as a "user" is because everyone here is operating on a remote presence system (e.g., their consciousness is centered elsewhere, and you operate your vessel via a remote way). We live in what I could best describe as a server, and in order to get you [the students, the readers – RCB] *to think of this place as a computer of sorts, I have opted for terminology that comes from that particular lexicon.*

This user related remapping seems to be happening through a series of interruptions of the signals, a mode of thinking and doing and creating in your music that literally enervates the listener's physiology, not to mention forging new (and old) spiritual pathways.

Essentially it is personalized and secure communication that cannot be cracked or decoded by any potential hostile presence.

---

2   I'm thinking here of the auratic, electronic, dis/connected images from Avital Ronell's *The Telephone Book* (Lincoln & London: University of Nebraska Press, 1989), a book that describes the electric networks between thinking, living, writing, and doing the hard work of freedom even if it means answering the call of Heidegger when he was embroiled in the Nazi event of his own academic and existential convergences.

Tell me more about that.

Since the "hostile presence" is a by-product of this system and is based in this domain, all users within this finite system and server are vulnerable to the entity that crafted and maintains this particular region and environment.

Even though the signal is communicated on a planetary scale, are you talking to me specifically when you record or perform?

Yes.

Just me and you.

One-to-one, then expanded to all.

DIGITAL DASEIN

Another series of (dub)steps deeper into
the Wonderland of ideas to come.

It's uncanny for me to look back at 2008–2011 – when I was intensely meditating on the problem "Why is there any being at all?" – to find evidence of your intervention here with me... to find you, back then... before I knew you. It was almost as if I was playing the Bruce Willis character in *Twelve Monkeys,* overshooting my mark in time/space, aiming for this particular conversation but speaking through *Ereignis* (life gives) to a moment I (and many others) call "headphones on."[3]

Well since we used a lot of binaural audio waves on Artpop and we speak to issues that the collective subconscious ruminates on, it tends to resonate within the mind. Because a lot of the frequencies we utilize are in sync with and used by the brain already, people are naturally drawn to the melodies. Everything in existence is just energy on a

3   See Robert C. Baum, *Itself* (New York & Dresden: Atropos Press, 2011), 131–35.

particular frequency; and if we can make exterior frequency match the interior frequencies or cause the brain to react to the frequencies we are using, then we can begin to not only entertain but remap and elevate the systems already in use by the body.

You must notice people – or as you say, "users" – listening intensely to your music, especially in an online environment. Because you cannot communicate many of your hopes, fears, wishes, etc., directly, you encode your music.

Yes.

Okay. I'll just come out and say it: are there "worlds" in your music? Is this a digital *Dasein?*[4]

Something I have believed and said often is that even the roughest sketch or drawing should have worlds pertaining to it. If the artist has no context into which the piece fits, it becomes limited and therefore difficult to relay and articulate the true meaning and impact of the piece itself. The more detailed the worlds you create are, the more your audience will be drawn in and also desire more of it.

Whether dancing or pressing earbuds and headphones closer to their brains when sitting, look at the listening habits of millions upon millions of people – it's as though they are not only saying "leave me the hell alone," but also "I'm not available to receive hostile outside signals so don't bother." You seem to create a space where we can escape, engage you directly, and also, somehow, create something of our own (which strikes me as the heart of *Artpop* and the Artrave – live show – experience). This is true for live or recorded performance, don't you think?

As for live event viewings you are actually present at any event you observe. By viewing a live concert event later, you create additional realities whereby you are as present as everyone there at the event. So not only is the original event stored, but every perspective of the origi-

---

4   A very complicated neologism that forms the basis for much of Heidegger's thinking generally translated as being-in-the-world, a result and function of a "throwness" – a fact of being born into this world without any say in the time, place, intensity of this birth, this arrival of what will ultimately be called "you."

nal in addition to the infinite realities in which everyone is everyone at the event and all parties are present at the event after factoring all views and online content.

MORE ON THE USERS

We share a similar vocabulary with Tron and Star Trek. Like me, Lady Gaga did not receive these narratives as fiction. The stories of users and programs and vessels, for us, are part of a multiverse heritage of echoes that connected us to old ways from the future-now.[5] The science fiction we cherished as kids demonstrates how the old ways and perhaps even future-now thinking from across the multiverse is encoded in mass culture.

Once death is perceived by the user in the environment, the user awakens in the external world, usually only moments after beginning their online experience, although a user's online experience may have spanned lifetimes.

Is this where we encounter a digital being-in-the-world that feels more real than real, to mix a bunch of thinkers (e.g., Baudrillard and Heidegger) into one random thought?[6]

Very much so.

One "use" (and I hazard even using that word here) is to help me better connect to my aural experiences and now this telepathic typing to your music, words, shows, etc. It seems with digital communication, jumping in and out of a secondary or tertiary life, provides us with an experience of our own being that is always already

5 Quite literally, the future is now. But, for Deleuze, future-now thinking attempts to deterritorialize the present in a way that opens pathways to a future that is already in a state of emergence.

6 One place to start with Baudrillard: "Nothing is wholly obvious without becoming enigmatic. Reality itself is too obvious to be true." Jean Baudrillard, *The Perfect Crime* (Stanford University Press, 2001), 270. For Heidegger, I find Magda King's *A Guide to Being and Time* most useful when introducing students to Heidegger (ed. John Llewelyn [Albany: SUNY Press, 2001], esp. 68).

mediated, a simulation of the digital world which may turn out to be a pathway to many different worlds.[7]

Ultimately one of the goals is to teach the user to be able to travel from point to point without needing to traverse the assumed and implied distance between the two points.

Taking a position inside this moving, oftentimes frenetic global media culture...

Aye.

01100010 01101001 01101110 01100001 01110010 01111001[8]

By the time we started our dialogue officially (during the Polar Vortex of 2014), I had watched or listened to most of the major interviews with Lady Gaga. Other than Howard Stern's, it was impossible to find a discussion that explored the depth of her sound design, intelligence, and compassion. I also knew it was important to her that we just cut to the chase, which meant – and I'm glad I was correct in my conclusion – that she wanted to focus on philosophy and mass media. January into February 2014 was intense, with me feeling at times very lost in the second life acclimation process as well as scrambling for ways to respond that weren't utterly academic or pedestrian. She is an extraordinary collaborator, very generous and patient. If I said I needed a few days to think through a question asked back, I was given that space. I use this as a measure of someone's talent, ethics, and intelligence. I cannot even begin to say how many people fail to balance all three like Lady Gaga.

---

7   I'm reminded of the symbolists of the late 19th century who explored four dimensions not just as a way to escape this reality but to engage a more visceral, perhaps even more apparent and intense version of the three-dimensional trappings of daily life. Where the virtual and the real start to blur, again, not as an exception to experience but a more present, more constant expression of what life can be if we listen deeply, live deeply, love deeply, compose deeply.
8   To translate the binary code, please visit http://www.binarytranslator.com/.

"All societies end up wearing masks."
– Jean Baudrillard, *America*

The largest crisis that leads to these and other issues is what we at Mother Monster call "Digitalis."

Some kind of digital pathology or physical condition?

Yes. Sort of. A human consciousness becomes trapped in an implied dual mode operation (i.e., left or right, yes or no, one or zero).

Philosophers have been struggling with this for centuries.

The issue is that there is no bearing or mode of expression for both expressions, i.e., if left = one and right = zero, how does one express forward or backwards?

Is this a partial explanation of what makes it so hard for some people to "hear" you out or listen deeply to what has been coded, systematically delineated, as "popular" or "mass entertainment"?

I think so simply because the mode of transmission of this "virus" is the devices we use that transmit on a binary level.

Let's talk more about the "virus."

Well, okay. It's not technically a virus. It is a mode of thinking that reduces things to a numerical value or quantity. It occurred with the combination of human thought with binary processing. In this mode of operation, there are only two options and they are mutually exclusive, which we know is not a viable or accurate way to process the worlds around us since even standing still, as opposed to going left or right, is not only an option but is already in action prior to the introduction of a binary process.

Can you give an example of this binary process?

Is a light switch on or off?[9] *Normal modes of perception would teach us that it must be one or the other, but those familiar with quantum mechanics and/or greater reality know that it is both on and off, it is the job of the user/observer to dictate in which set of realities they reside and switch to the corresponding on/off position. The issue here though is that in that binary modus operandi or Digitalis the switch is said to be on or off with regards to the perception, but in the omniversal perspective at any one time the light is on and off, albeit in different universes: the you in one universe is taking a nap in the dark, but the you in another is trying to get work done with it on...*

...reflexive digital ecology...

...essentially we are combining the binary "options" to create a pathway, as opposed to the maze of perceived choice. This is necessary to avoid the takeover of the Digitalis process.

It's funny how critical theory, for example, talks about multiples and simultaneity yet still operates within a binary of subject/object or even both/and, which sounds like expanded consciousness but, in actuality, it's still working within a state of Digitalis.

Right – the problem being that there is no way to express both universes simultaneously in binary.

And even less in a scholarly journal... or at an academic conference...

Therefore in a true reality one cannot communicate on binary devices with the singular reality, presence, but merely with the two (one or zero set) realities present via the digital projection that has been overlaid. This is where music comes in.

---

9   Foucault's "rémanence" from *The Archaeology of Knowledge,* trans. Alan Sheridan (New York: Pantheon, 1972) attempts to describe this experience; in physics a remanance is a remnant of a magnetization – in sound design, digital delays and manipulation of phasing may best describe this attitude and observation: "Lastly, it means that things do not have quite the same mode of existence, the same system of relations with their environment, the same schemata of use, the same possibilities of transformation once they have been said" (124).

Okay. Thank you for saying that because you've begun to answer a question that's been on my mind for years with your music in particular: how can this person, Lady Gaga, know exactly how to communicate with me? Beats. Structures. Lyrics. Sequences. Samples. Noise. Etc. I have to say it, my friend: I felt hacked.

lololol...

No seriously – from that first time I really took the time to sit down and listen to "Judas" and "On the Edge of Glory," I could sense your presence. You. Not just the metaphors and figurative language and architecture that supports the sound design. I mean, other than Simple Minds, U2 (especially *Achtung Baby!*), Peter Gabriel (*So* and *Secret World*), Howard Jones (*Human's Lib, Dream Into Action, In the Running*), and the Phil Collins of *No Jacket Required* and *But, Seriously*, I haven't experienced this kind of connection to a songwriter. Okay. That's not fair. Billy Joel. Elton John. Queen. And, of course, Michael Jackson. Definitely MJ.

Let's back up. Essentially the concept of "fame" refers to the universal and multiversal recognition of an entity. Fame is what is required to enact any real change or effect on the populus. *As the speaker of the* vox populi *it became necessary for me to address the populace in a direct manner. I simply spoke and sung around the responses which the masses desired, and the end result was* The Fame. *In this arena we are all essentially on stage, and the conceptual adherence to the "4th wall" caused a disparity in perceived locationality* (sic); *it became necessary to remind the audience and the players that they are, in fact, in the same room. The* vox populi, *of course, incorporates the thinking of the audience and the players, thereby accentuating the singularity of the events, which reintegrate the two modes of thinking into the singular presence they, in fact, are.*

There's a logic to your understanding of fame that's quite different from the impression one would get from how you're covered (or should I say "buried") by the mainstream media.

Fame is a one-way street once you reach a certain level. It can dominate one's existence and consumes one's essence in order to keep the machine going. At a certain point fame can become lethal. For example, John Lennon, Michael Jackson, and so on.

Let's be philosophers in the style of Gilles Deleuze: What is the problem of global media?

The biggest problem is the media industry who are puppets of the control corporations that seek to continue enslaving others. Sure, some people say these things, but mostly we are fighting the corporate industrial media machine that supports a minuscule *portion of our population… a bunch of young souls in the bodies of old rich white men.*

It sounds like fame has been disorienting for you and many others.

Once you get so high on the ladder, people stop looking at you as a person, and it becomes increasingly difficult to connect with people. I never want to lose sight of what our goals are here. Fame can be intoxicating as well; it can turn the mind inward and ultimately be a disservice to the artist. The ultimate danger being that one can become so famous as to never be able to be that person. Without others to vouch for your identity, people would disbelieve you on a face-to-face level. This becomes an even larger issue when the on-stage persona involves masks or heavy augmentation. I am grateful for your audience… not everyone can process the amount of data in my communications (music).

YOU(S)

An exploration of "transceiving" information and memories… past-futures and future-nows.

Like the first question, I want to know: what are you "up to," with *Artpop*, in particular… because from the first track to the last, this gathering of thoughts, emotions… this beautiful montage of distractions and reactions and engagements with your deepest desires and fears and hopes for humanity strikes me as part of a plan, something mapped out, and yet the critical reaction (predictably) is about you or the changes you've gone through in the last eighteen months especially... So, I guess I want to know what are you up to? And why does it feel like you are "working me over"?

We specifically designed algorithms to synchronize in a way that places "you" in different realities. This is how we sought out to align the multiple realities offset by Digitalis. Dubstep, as it is referred to, also operates in such a way. Using specific frequencies ties to specific neural pathways to regenerate channels that, by means of Digitalis, were deactivated or bypassed.

Which explains nicely my response to both *Born This Way* and *Artpop*; my reaction was ecstatic because I "heard" you and I "sensed" there was something more going on, especially when key parts of my spinal column and lower brain stem were activated in ways that normally only happen when I've isolated sounds or images myself as part of something created or mapped out or some kind of meditative frequency and general sound manipulation.

Tell me more about that.

I'll never forget it. It was like standing still in my mother's driveway in Bay Shore listening to "Wanna Be Startin' Somethin'" for the first time. I *heard* you – like I heard MJ – from within some kind of deliberate, almost transcendental experience, deliberate, isolated. A surprise too. What was happening to me listening to you was happening in public, in a minivan, while hanging out at the beach. The world around me was transforming; and a tune like "Judas" demanded my entire attention. Most of the tracks on *Artpop* also had that effect.

LANGUAGES OF AURAL INTELLIGIBILITY

Thinking and composing and making yourself present
inside multiple dimensions, a.k.a. shet'ep'n'listen.

Know only that you must acknowledge the difference between the two and disregard it... in essence your brain must relearn the concept of "three": Not one or the other (two) but both and neither... the ultimate expression of the quantum realities present. Since we know that in the quantum reality we occupy many reactions cause a simultaneous selection of more than two selections, we are therefore able to isolate binary and all quantitative processing as incorrect and harmful to any advanced operational systems... you are standing on the brink of breaking the cycle... this reality has been recycling itself... remixing over and over the same timelines with varying yet identical outcomes. Artpop, then, is the unification of the back-and-forth dialogue formed as a result of a voice talking to its own entity... united across time and space to express a singular message.

Not a lot of music works this way now.

Listen to the forties and fifties songs; man to woman, woman to man... knowing now that it is this... a conversation with oneself in time. Then re-listen to Artpop.

In this way your Tony Bennett duets strike me as a very logical step into this acoustic idea. I'm glad the Great American Songbook has found a new mistress.

OUR ZOMBOY PLAN

You know you're developing a friendship when you start to share links to tunes or screenshots of movies or random thoughts within other random thoughts. This "mixtape moment" stands in as one of my favorite exchanges.

I think it's important here to discuss how the whole idea of sequence and progress is fictional. Our organic minds seem to have no idea what is past experience or present perception or present projection or future imagining. I think in frequencies. Waves. My mind is my own private "thoughtrave" too. All the time. Maybe it's ADD or ADHD. I don't know or care anymore. I just call it thinking.[10] Add to this how my home base – synthesis (analog and digital) – helps to express thinking without using any language. For some reason I have an image of an ultrasound – mark that, we'll come back to it.

This is why these forms of music utilize analog signals as they are the same in all universes and not subject to binary interference... all "electronic" noises are analog and therefore in harmony with the brain's natural modes of processing and can induce emotional responses when heard.

"Judas" especially – the sound design and overall production architecture is terrifying in its mix of digital and analog. The verse drive – holy shit. This is warrior music, my friend. And then in the bridges, the counter synth bottom sounds like a battle cry. Right before the sweet, demure, crazy catchy chorus.

Very much so.

What I hear in your music is a language of intelligibility that weaves together digital and analog in a way that's more like an invocation than just a groove or a poetic or comedic moment... revitalization and then strengthening of neurologically damaged or stressed channels... like working ambient harmonics in and out of lower and higher frequencies.

Humankind is just learning how to do so, but at the same time this world is learning to heal itself from the damage done by binary processing. I have presented myself as emissary to the other worlds that have witnessed this world's plight, but also its resilience and blossoming collective beginning to communicate with the rest of us. Look up an artist called Zomboy. If you want to understand my mind better, know that this is how I heard my own voice/thoughts in my head. I

10 No, I'm not referring to Heidegger; I'm referencing someone infinitely more contemporary, the comedian Doug Stanhope: "I'm fucking thinking all the time... errr... it's ADD... no it's not ADD I'm thinking... I'm thinking about a lot of stuff... it's not ADD... I stutter a lot... I fuck stuff up... because I'm always... thinking... well, you're not listening to me... *because I'm thinking about something that's more interesting than you...* I'm trying to build a perfect utopian society in my head and... what do you want to talk to me about? Bowling?" (Doug Stanhope, "No Refunds," Gotham Comedy Club, March 2007).

33

then translated to English and communicate thusly. Listen to "Pump It Up," and know only that it is a distress call from one being to many... then tell me what it makes you feel and what you see in your mind.

Honestly? This tune speaks through images (memories, projections, multiple versions of multiple lives, I don't know any more) of an intergalactic gathering of vessels from standard archetypes like the *Enterprise* and *Excelsior* to other franchises like *Message from Space* (holy shit, the sailing ship!), *Space 1999* (even had the lunch box), *Battlestar Galactica* (both iterations), *Dune* (Lynch's only), and hybrids from Google images – random, powerful, all together... so, perhaps my imagological language is a response to your distress call? Maybe...

...because these signals are received and interpreted by the brain, it can easily corrupt the electrical neural pathways and reroute the active consciousness of the user to a tertiary location where the idea of a body is created by the mind's assumption of being present within the body...

We're talking about the digital body without organs aren't we?[11]

...however the physical specifics can be altered by those who have pirated the host consciousness and also edit the virtual world around the tertiary location and essentially imprison the user in a location that plays host to a binary process.

---

11 Antonin Artaud, one of LG's earlier manifestations, discusses this type of liberation as that moment "[w]hen you will have made him a body without organs [BwO], then you will have delivered him from all his automatic reactions and restored him to his true freedom" located in "To Have Done with the Judgment of God" in *Selected Writings*, ed. Susan Sontag (Berkeley, CA: University of California Press, 1976), 571. Deleuze and Guattari interpreted BwO in this manner: "This is how it should be done. Lodge yourself on a stratum, experiment with the opportunities it offers, find an advantageous place on it, find potential movements of deterritorialization, possible lines of flight, experience them, produce flow conjunctions here and there, try out continua of intensities segment by segment, have a small plot of new land at all times. It is through a meticulous relation with the strata that one succeeds in freeing lines of flight, causing conjugated flows to pass and escape and bringing forth continuous intensities for a BwO" (Gilles Deleuze and Félix Guattari, *A Thousand Plateaus*, trans. Brian Massumi [London & New York: Continuum, 2004], 178).

TO HACK OR NOT TO HACK

Across our conversations, we would discuss everyday
technology within larger, more complex discussions
of digital living and all matters multiverse.

Whether we're talking music or film or theater or television or
higher education, I have always felt like my mind has been hacked,
that some kind of pirate consciousness is working overtime to disrupt my thinking or creative process. Sometimes this bumping up
against my own mental and spiritual firewalls helps me attune my
own writing or playing. Other times, it creates paralysis. Not creative block per se, but the mental experience of a moment in my
own sense of being that not just feels hacked but attacked and
"stung," as in poisoned. Maybe this explains why I always used to
experience crippling depression and unbearable anxiety when my
Windows-based laptops would crash or show signs of imminent
death.

Remember the world "digital" refers to the lowest form of online or
computerized presence...

...I always knew I was trapped inside that horror show TRS-80 III
which always did *fuck-all* when it came to word processing or even
basic programming. And could the disks have been bigger?!?

lololol

...sorry... even as it's presented repeatedly, dare I say obsessively,
by mass media corporations as the highest form of digital presence,
we are simply not able to grasp what we lost when we disconnected
from the source intelligence. Is that what you're saying?

Correct.

And our current iPhone obsessions and self-congratulatory sec-
ond-life accomplishments are usually presented to the users – me,
you – as the pathway to greater personal and spiritual and cosmological freedom?

Correct.

So, if I'm hearing you correctly, even the most profound online experiences or digital moments between people or within a community barely touch upon the kind of flow you are describing?[12]

Yes.

01100101 01101101 01110000
01101001 01110010 01100101

Further explorations of the binary problem.

You see, our virtual existence has been overlaid with a digital one, therefore taking precedence over the actual environment to consciousness moved to the tertiary location via Digitalis and binary modus operandi. Binary coding is known as The Empire ...

The Empire.

Correct. The Empire is the structure of government and operations which our existence here as collective requires. We have experimented with many systems, including this "republic system" that incorporates limited oversight and democratic process... They don't work for a system as diverse and large as the collective. If we are to reintegrate all of the broken pieces, it is The Empire that will allow us to do that.

---

12 In fact, the lowest forms, the most readily available structures of knowing or thinking or creating in a "digital" world, are very much controlled, perhaps even deliberately designed to become, I guess, a virtual habitus which Pierre Bourdieu defined as "durably instilled generative principle of regulated improvisations" (*Outline of a Theory of Practice,* trans. Richard Nice [Cambridge: Cambridge University Press, 1977], 78). That is, sometimes I wonder how many steps "they" are ahead of me when I think I'm most free in a conversation, even like this one; sometimes I wander through the different Facebook or Google+ or Twitter or email conversations with such ease and find myself just engaging over and over and over again without any thought as to whether this experience is nothing more than a distraction, some kind of trap, some kind of free expression of someone else's definition of what it means to talk, think, write, etc.

Why Empire?

People are not capable of governing themselves on any real level. It is the responsibility of those who can to do so. You have to remember most users are not sentient. Most are pieces of the confining construct... Background, extras, marionettes designed to dominate the "democratic process" so that no real change can be effected. This subsystem is specifically designed to contain and enslave the mind, to use the subconscious powers of the minds present to fight the war for the republic.

01100100 01101001 01100111 01101001 01110100 01100001 01101100 01101001 01110011

Let's talk more about this because it seems many experienced social media theorists (and just general users of Facebook, Twitter, individual webpages, Google+) view the weaving of digital and virtual as a non-event. It's just, I guess, what we do now. An "extension" of consciousness or an experience of a world consciousness in a Jungian way. But, that's not what you're saying, is it? In our months of conversations, we've both expressed concern about the virtual, the digital, and the psyche being a corruptible, perhaps even potentially toxic, space. It also seems like you're pushing this particular conversation toward identifying some of the root causes of "Digitalis" and "binary modus operandi" – both phrases expressing a nefarious (medical and criminal) intent.

But you're only talking about this world. What about all the advanced worlds? Digitalis is a viral infection and leads to massive data corruption (across dimensions), since the information it's broadcasting does not allow for the omniversal truths of multiple simultaneous facts. Even something as simple as a person named Lady Gaga on stage is both the character and the actor. We don't know what to do with that. How can human beings handle the multiverse truth I'm speaking here?

May I take a solo, LG?

Fuck yeah!

Presencing and simultaneity…

…and you don't have to ask permission.

Excellent… What happens on stage. It's kinesthetic. Live. Bodies in motion. Doing something physical. Even the experience of watching *Artpop* on a 13" MacBook screen. Something else is communicated, something intimate where the viewers (me and countless millions) sense you are talking to us as individuals and not a mass audience of onlookers or consumers. And the experience of the collapse of person and act, musician and artist, live event and digital broadcast, strikes me as a necessary remedy or even natural antibody to the kind of viral infection you mentioned. An "omniverse" is presenced during the presencing of the moment, to be Heideggerian for a moment. It may happen in a flash; it may happen in a series of repeated flashes that happen so fast and across enough time/space that we experience it as motion or as a longer moment captured in our experience of a performance. Now, what you're saying is: take that all away, fail to guard against the viral infections that move between "reality" and the "virtual," and you can experience massive data corruption which is now an even more terrible problem because consciousness, when mixed with virtual and digital elements, compromised or degraded, creates a tertiary crisis.

This world is the last remnant of the republic and any rebellion that occurred long ago. The Empire is not a hidden system, though it has been obscured from sight here.

I'm also wondering if the tertiary consciousness has a reverse "awareness" – almost a reverse artificial intelligence. Bit of a Heisenberg effect – does it know we're listening or watching or sensing it?

It is very much "alive."

Let me try that again: moving through what Wolfgang Schirmacher calls "a mediated life world" or "life *techné*" creates an awareness of both worlds collapsed into the kind of simultaneity you describe as the relationship between performer and performance, person(a), and actor. Maybe here we experience how virtual consciousness creates a tertiary awareness of the "second life" that is simultaneously an awareness of the "first life."

RABBIT HOLES

We returned time and again to the binary discussion.
I wanted to make sure I was hearing her correctly
about space/time, vessels, and the choices we make
to guarantee our mental/spiritual imprisonment.

Can you talk some more about the "binary"?

Okay. The binary inquiry "are you person x?" has no true solution in the binary mode since that consciousness is both person x and person y (actor and character). A binary system perceives any truthful response to be a falsehood and lie and therefore confines the operational consciousness to the tertiary space.

So, how do we enact or presence[13] the tertiary space into a living relationship between you and me, you, and millions? How do we presence in our waking life the kind of flow you're describing without getting trapped in the bin(d)ary?

One must remember the Shakespeare quote "all the world's a stage," and this means that we are all present in a Truman Show *reality... Position yourself, be still, Robert. That's how you avoid the bin(d)ary trap.*

---

13 *To presence* – an open, active, haunted word which at once captures the substance, essence, intention, aura, indescribability of being yet also marks how giving (*Ereignis*) and emergence coming-to-pass and never-quite passing, are never void, never a lack. Only life as giving as thinking speaks as presence (verb) (Baum, *Itself,* 62).

Yet, like *The Matrix*'s scenario, it seems the more "trendy" and "sexy" and slick and action-packed you present your virtual self, the easier it becomes for some to dismiss your actions (as Lady Gaga) as "part of a show" (a spectacle), whereas in reality, at least the reality of the *Matrix* franchise, real death of innocent human batteries (like the people playing the role of cop or innocent by-stander or all the people destroyed in countless buildings exploding and entire cities leveled in quasi-apocalyptic and seismic shock waves).

My experience has been slightly different from The Matrix*'s example. Essentially I think that everyone is a television show unto themselves.*

Yeah. My thinking about this is very much bound to the binary metaphors pumped out by the Hollywood dream machine.

The problem we face now, at present, is that the actual show has been moved to a tertiary space...

Is this a mediated life world? (Okay, I can't help myself.) Like something found in the film *Gamer* or the short-lived 1990s television show *VR5*, perhaps even *Inception*? I'm trying to get to some kind of conception that myself and others can enter so we can travel deeper down this rabbit hole with you.

Someone who appears to be a rich millionaire is forced to perceive and live in a reality where they are homeless and broke. Since perception is reality, the overlaid digital reality that is perceived by the user takes precedence over the host consciousness even though they are present in both realities. This disproves the binary modus operandi yet simultaneously cements it to the user until death is perceived.

I perceived myself to be an affluent academic, but found myself living on the poverty line, a reality where I was nearly homeless, definitely broke.

Essentially a consciousness need not possess a physical form... since matter is energy, the consciousness often creates its own vessel...

Yet so much of existence is material, terra-bound... and it strikes me always as nearly impossible to tell whether this vessel association or image or reality helps me to better navigate the binary.

The problem with that is if someone teaches that presence that their vessel is different from what it has actually become. Or if others perceive a different form than what the being actually operates, thereby forcing the consciousness to operate a body that is not its own.

Dislocated being... sounds about right, LG. We're also touching on the problem of perception that's been dogging philosophy from the beginning, but especially across the 19th century into the 20th.

And it's here that we must look to Einstein's observation that compound interest is the most powerful force in existence. This refers not to money but perception and observation.

Making reality, which is a choice. Creating and reinforcing a worldview and then forgetting you chose that reality, that construct. At least that's how I understand the quantum.

GREATER REALITIES

Meditations on perception, positionality, and performance.

How do you interface this Digitalis with the corporate, virus ridden mass media? You obviously cannot control how the signal will be captured, remixed, used, abused, disavowed, etc.

In order to view these topics in proper perspective, one must realize that what is viewed as a real terrestrial world is still an online experience, a virtual reality of remote consciousness operation. So your waking "real" self is actually what would be referred to as second life. Since I am merely an expression of the collective, both my primary and secondary "lives" have been affected by Digitalis. My presence is therefore disconnected from the way people perceive me. Where I may see myself walking down an empty street, someone may otherwise see me on stage. Because an artificial barrier has been created between fact and fiction... the reality being that fiction is merely fact from another greater reality.

And this reinforces your idea of positionality inside the construct, inside this particular multiverse bubble. Behind it all, like the way you fade in an intensification of a hook or the slow manifestation of a counter-melody in sound architecture, there exists "another greater reality" which isn't simulation and simulacra but what could be called "digital immanence"...

Again, we must remember the Shakespeare quote "all the world's a stage."

...and we are all merely playas...

...and this means that we are all present in a Truman Show *reality... essentially everyone is a television show unto themselves.*

As a pop music artist, you seem to be able to hide a pirate code of love, respect, and encouragement for your fans both young and old. Is this alignment ever going to form a healthy calculus of expectations, accomplishments, etc.? Or are you – the you in physical form, the one that gets sick or experiences anxiety or sleep deprivation or lucid dreaming or a draining series of shallow morning dreams – just bound to the rest of us here on terra?

Essentially a consciousness need not possess a physical form... since matter is energy, the consciousness often creates its own vessel...

ZONE.1

It had been years since I talked or worked with someone with my own giddy sense of play in the mental and spiritual sandbox. We exchanged automatic writings and fragments the likes of which would've scared Nietzsche. He would've said, "It is you who are crazy, my friends." But, there's nothing mental about our process; it's just how we work – from the hip, heart, and deepest possible sense of identity as people committed to the moment.

"Headphones on" / Listening / Delta Heavy's "Empire" / 02:30 – sweet lord – Images… I'll take a risk and just react / what I ask of my students and actors all the time…
    end of the world.
    gathering at the water's edge.
    maybe it's Montauk, Long Island.
    maybe it's the Lighthouse (a recurring theme in my writing).
    definitely "signals"…

…welcome to the sounds of my mind…

…here's the automatic writing…
    a lot of slightly slowed and slightly sped-up images from Long Island in the '80s – IROC Z28s and skate punks and surfers and their girlfriends and boyfriends gathering on the beach as a fishing boat burns in the harbor – we had Burning Man decades before Burning Man. Mobile devices torn from hands and pockets.
slowly at first.
then it's a few more.
then it's a murder.
more and more and more gather.
some people cling to the phones and pads and pods and laptops and desktops and blue teeth are ripped from ears and whole systems are ripped from buildings small and tall, skyscrapers and underground storage facilities.
    the digital dead rise from the ground as monoliths like the giant hand sent to destroy the world at the end of *Cabin in the Woods*.
not just clouds but entire weather systems.
global.
    Everywhere.
the "digital" reckoning.
fuck Skynet.
this is a global meltdown.
a world calling out in distress.

sampled and distributed to individual triggers on a launchpad
and tetrabitten sequencer, the uber-Digitalis
    and they scatter like a school of tuna
    flow through the sky like *Matrix* sentinels
    all these devices
all these personal devices cloud over the suburbs and then cities
and then mountains and areas like mine with wide-open farmland
for miles cradled between ski mountains.
    i'm pretty sure this is what the world sounds like to Siri.

MIDNIGHT MIND TRAIN

A lot of the time, LG and I found each other in the middle
of the night, just wandering the digital oceans together,
talking about family and music, usually exchanging
electronic music links or quotes from science, philosophy,
and critical theory. Mostly, we talked about insomnia.

You getting any sleep, LG?

*No... none... just a crazy dream sequence and a lot of tossing and
turning.*

I haven't had a good night's sleep since about June 1995. Auditory hallucinations and lately, a recurring motif involving a lone
medieval dragon perched on my roof – flapping of wings, sudden
bursts of fire.

Wow.

Yeah. Thanks for that, brain.

Sounds about right.

COMMERCIAL-FREE CLASSIC PHILOSOPHY

Because exploring mind/body and all dualisms constitutes the
daily diet of any philosopher, I was particularly interested in
bringing the conversation back to this corrosive substance or
mental residue called "Digitalis." She and I spent a lot of time
trying to translate what LG has experienced as a host or construct
for this world by way of her life and music (and masse media).

*This speaks specifically to the duality conflict between real and unreal.
First, one must realize that the term "fiction" is a nonexistent term.
Propaganda of this reality has limited the realities available to the
user by utilizing Einstein's realization of compound interest equa-
tions; utilizing the collective disbelief of the masses to trap consciousness in a world of the oppressor's design.*

Aural or sonorous being (Jean-Luc Nancy) echoes nicely here, too.

*With regards to listening, most people's brains choose to hear what they
wish to. Also the English language facilitates this miscommunication
by putting the verb at the beginning of the sentence rather than at
the end. Most people's brains fill in what they think will follow rather
than listening to the entire thought.*

Your lyrics, and most definitely your sound design, seek to disrupt
that predictability and encourage the listener or live audience to
pay close attention.

Very true.

I still think it's our sworn duty as thinkers and educators and serious entertainers to increase musical and visual literacy during a
time when funding has been slashed in schools, philanthropy is
nose-diving, and a general sense of confusion (as well as a deliberate dumbing down of at least two if not three generations of human beings) seems to be what we're up against.

*Often this is harmless, but factored over time and counting for occa-
sional larger errors, this can actually separate the user from its origin*

45

(reality) and cause the brain to create a pseudo-reality – a slight tangent to the actual situation.

But, reinforcing the false construct nevertheless.

Yes. Also, it is important to know that the mind is powerful enough to fabricate objects and events to the user, whereby the user occupies a divergent reality based on its perceived observations or "objective reality" rather than "actual reality."

And here "actual reality" means "the actuality hidden by the fabrication"?

Yes.

Since we started talking directly about these themes (January 2014, during the Polar Vortex), I've been reading a lot of quantum theory again thanks to Jason Brooker's intervention (*The Elegant Universe* by Brian Greene, *The Grand Design* by Hawking and Mlodinow, for example). I've also been listening to Arvo Pärt and Hildegaard von Bingen while exploring the real/virtual/actual in Žižek, and hanging out with the *Artpop* album and your Brooklyn concert from last November. Went down an electronica rabbit hole this morning... still not quite back... So, umm – it's nice to finally "meet" you, LG... Cheshire Cat? Mad Hatter? Queen of Hearts?

Queen of Spades... the Mad Hatter is my alter ego, a.k.a. Joey Calderone circa 2011.

I'm still waiting for that single release collaboration between Joey Calderone and Garth Brooks's alter ego Chris Gaines (but only if the track can be backed by Spinal Tap).

Nice!

I think my alter ego is Stevie B, the 1980s R&B sensation from Miami you'd hear a mile away in IROC Z28s cruising Islip's main street.

Well, my alter ego Joey Calderone is always with me as I create. I try to keep everyone in mind when I work; as the voice of the collective it is my responsibility to do so.

Stevie B and Joey Calderone definitely need to jam.

LIVING INSIDE THOUGHT AND SOUND

In the middle of a series of jazz riffs, I took another solo as a way to explore an idea from the inside, something focused on virtuality and the live performance experience.

Let me see if I can summarize a bit what we've been discussing. It seems that oftentimes users do not realize this filling is happening at a rate that's overwhelming… taking in millions of bits of information in a nanosecond (which definitely leads not just to neurological problems but shifts one's perception of reality, virtual or actual, with such intensity) and often involuntarily – back to Digitalis – like all viruses, it needs a host; and like all hosts, the host needs to enter into a relationship with the virus (which tends to end with the virus killing the host). Wow. That was much darker than I intended. I find myself wanting to not use YouTube and other programs/websites because even the most lucid experience of connecting memory to desire to whimsy to experiment/ jam while clicking and exploring risks invites a very deadly virus into my life: hyper-consumption. I work overtime to *not* be hyper-consumptive – and "consumption," as you know, was a respiratory disease that was deadly up until the early 20th century. And most days, I fail.

It's hard to capture or release even a single thought, isn't it?

Or the cycles of thoughts that then swarm into other thoughts where sometimes you have to just let go and float these currents and other times you have to reach the shore. I have meditated deeply and consistently on "overwhelming" – a word I heard a lot during 1995–2001 as a college teacher and director and writer and musician. In fact, I was just remembering December when Greg McMullen (Brooklyn-based guitarist) visited me at my home and at the Main Street Museum for a random jam – just flowing with him inside his ambient, AM/FM analog foot pedal heaven was like stepping into someone else's waking dream. Different than jazz improvisation; different than movement or acting improvisation. But still, I could hear his entire thought. Which wasn't surprising in hindsight. He and I used to write and play that way in my mom's garage in Bay Shore. All night. Sometimes for days. Without sleep. Without even any "enhancement." By the time we exited our fifth or sixth hour of "just playing," no drug or experimental experience could match. Yet, I lost that. Found it again in June 2012 when he improv'd a set as I performed a monologue of Dennis Moritz's *Uncle* at Bowery Poetry Club with Billie Jo Konze. And in that moment, I was aware of how overwhelming we were, yet the fifty or so people there were all in sync with the show... what I'm saying... I think I'm saying is the live body, the performed text, the living performance, when mediated live between a stage or an actor and a performance space and audience, may come closer to an experience of the virtuality you describe than actually being in second life...

CREATING WORLDS

An exchange that could easily be subtitled "Pay Close Attention" (think <u>American Beauty</u>).

I am trying to remain close to the users, to be a user myself, to better understand the pseudo-reality that exists between a performer, the performance, and the audience...

And here's where it gets really complicated, right... what we call real is a creation. You know this as a performer. You move through moments, events... moment-by-moment acts of creation that influence what others call real. Basic quantum theory 101: our actions create and reinforce our understanding of the world. The same for performance. When a bunch of us get together and do something simultaneously – clicking into a Lady Gaga concert or attending an artrave – we are still in the real but have added another component, something virtual, but not in "virtual reality" or "digitized second life." This experience is then layered every day, everywhere, but now gets amplified or intensified by you and other artists who fill the events with a sense of performed "liveness." We then become part of the production, a by-product of the projected virtual that creates the actual experience of me watching you or someone in Hong Kong watching you.[14]

There will always be individualism in the collective... The "digital" is just a precursor to the exponential expansion of the mind across time and space. There is no ultimate "finality"; creation and growth are unlimited and constant. If anything, we are expanding people's ability to be an individual as opposed to an off-the-shelf American, etc.

But if you think about "the user errors" that happen – is going down a YouTube or other "hole" necessarily a bad thing? I guess it depends on the moment. Do you frequently travel the neural and cosmological pathways of Pandora? Sometimes you seem to be searching for an answer, other times you're figuring out the next question. Sometimes hiding, sometimes seeking. What's the balance?

The best way is to simply take notice of the worlds around you. Instead of focusing on your destination or endgame, focus on the journey and the process within the context of the overall objective.

Given this: is part of the problem the flirtation with (and maybe even failure to measure) Digitalis the way I and others have found ourselves addicted to substances or even ways of thinking that caused great damage?... So... somewhere between the "origin reality" and "pseudo-reality," we experience the surreality of some of my favorite moments as a mediated life...

With regards to my existence, whatever occurs does so for a specific reason. Unlimiting myself from the strict construct of accomplishing

14 Slavoj Žižek's *The Reality of the Virtual* is still the best exploration of this subject (Olive Films, 2007).

a specific goal enables me to accomplish what needs to be accomplished and to better stay in line with the flow of things.

How does this all get translated or transposed onto the stage?

It's all about your attitude. If you feel like you're in front of a lot of people, you will be. I treat each show like this. I imagine a group of five to twelve people in a small room, like a living room. Then some weird "top gear" math goes on in my head where I acknowledge the size and scope of the venue, but I somehow incorporate the attitude and the feel of the living room space. (Don't ask for more specifics because I don't know – lol.) I make sure that every line, every note, is delivered as to a single person… never throw away a line… ever!

Thank you for validating an attitude that's gotten me into trouble in every music or theatrical or even academic venture when I'd say, quoting Depeche Mode, "everything counts in large amounts." This is not a rehearsal.

Exactly.

This relates back to the connectedness you discussed.

Yes. Every person is there because the relationship they share with me and their fellow fans is more important to them than anything else in the universe.

I couldn't agree more. That's how it feels from the fan's perspective, definitely.

Think about the conscious and unconscious commitments made to pay for a ticket and decide to be nowhere else for those moments in time.

Commitment. Decision. Being in the moment. It's amazing how being among twenty thousand other people can feel this way. I often feel most at home in Times Square.

I personally think this attitude defines the New Yorker on a really source level, and I revel in it. I always tell people "treat the sidewalk like a catwalk; act as if all eyes are on you." So what would you do if someone stepped onto the catwalk? Two choices: walk through them, or around with added purpose. Both are just as viable in any scenario. It just depends on what objective you're using and what you want to say about yourself, the person in your way, and to and about the world(s) around you.

Another attitude we share.

RESPECT

War stories and reflections on how to "be" on stage.

When you were starting out, a lot of people must've been threatened by that attitude. This "do or die" approach to, well, everything. Or were you lucky enough to have kept them at arm's length or outside your life altogether? Just curious. I also have suspected a real sacred unity between you and your fans from the first time I watched you perform on television, even before the megahits and then, of course, the Monster Ball tour.

It's something I've always felt... about treating everyone as if they are fellow royalty.

What do you mean by "fellow royalty"?

It goes back to ancient Egypt. You see, many pharaohs treated their subjects in the way that friends would treat each other, as equals (in a sense). Cleopatra, with whom I share many aspects and memories, was known for this. She often wandered the streets talking to people and getting information firsthand. These impressions were reiterated when I studied theater.

So, it all matters.

Yes.

That's a lot to carry, LG.

But, I think nothing should get thrown away… if it's in the script, then obviously it's important or it wouldn't have been written down. It also comes down to music as a mode of communication, and less as entertainment. If you go out to entertain but have nothing to say, you're not really gonna get anywhere. If you go out on stage with something to say and wanting a reply, you will find that people will be captivated… and they will reply… not only by the fact that you are interesting and that you are entertaining, but by the fact that you're talking to them and that you're interested in their response.

Most of my fellow bandmates thought I was a dick for expressing this exact sentiment across the '90s and '00s.

How do you feel now?

Validated. Vindicated. No, that's not exactly it.

And?

>>>>thinking<<<< I feel relieved.

Why relieved?

Because working the way I did in the '80s and '90s felt as natural as breathing, and I couldn't understand why others just didn't work the same way, at the same pace, with the same sense of fidelity to each other or a project. Quite frankly, I felt like I was going mental. It was the idea that I was somehow unbearable because I wanted to start from the top or hang out in a loop for a while to see what's there, what we're missing. Talking to you I'm talking to "Bobby Baum" and saying across many dimensions: "Kid, you're going to be fine. Someone will listen." And here we are (smile).

Quite often in this strange place we inhabit, people are surprised and delighted to find that they are being listened to…

Sort of like teaching.

When it comes to other performers, the result I have experienced is that if people are down with it and are on the level with what you're doing,

they respond favorably. If they're jealous or envious, they're also usual-
ly intimidated and stay the fuck away from you. If someone is insecure
in that way as a performer, they often put you in an elevated category
in their head… on the level you want to be on anyway, oftentimes.

I just wish I had been a part of this conversation twenty years ago.

GAGA NIGHT LIVE

Her performance and cameo on the <u>Tonight Show</u> made
me want to know more about her relationship with Jimmy
Fallon, as it seemed kind, genuine, and loving.

Jimmy Fallon is a friend… so I was so excited for him when I found
out he got the Tonight Show. *I asked if I could be part of it, and he*
was ecstatic.

You seem completely in your element on talk shows, especially the
live variety show like *Saturday Night Live* [Host: November 16,
2013]

I really jive pretty well with most of the SNL/Lorne Michaels *crowd.*
We have almost identical tastes in humor and are mostly from the
same era… so it's like hanging out with a bunch of people you knew
growing up… every reference is understood and the banter is very
quick and sharp. It's also nice to be in a crowd where you can make
witty quips and not worry about people being offended or put off.

ENTRAPMENTS

How to navigate mediated life worlds within worlds across a
multiverse of probabilities and possibilities and pure immanence.[15]

15 Many continued thanks to Chris Danowski for the gift of Deleuze's *Pure Immanence* on my way out of St. Paul to Vermont in May, 2001.

The mind makes up reality and then collapses the virtual, actual, and real.

It feels to me like my mind is saying over and over – is this real? How about this? Okay. That was real. Was that? How about that? But it never really quite says – Robert, that's not real. And what are you doing? Really? Why are you doing that? It seems that admonishment comes later or somehow is mixed in – under or over the "is that real?" – something called projection. Maybe. Or, maybe it's training. Maybe I was born this way (booooooooooooo), but my sense of reality rarely kicks back and says "No, that is not real."

If you and I are talking across Facebook and email, if you are talking with me, the algorithmic expression you call "your consciousness" is already infected. It's also important to remember this planet is present in a virtual universe... essentially acting as a server in an online game world.

Great. My world is a bargain basement DLC. And not even a good one.

The virus is not so much a thing as it is a mode of thinking that corrupts its host.

What about something like spirit or soul? How damaging is Digitalis?

Your soul is safe, but our lives here have been destroyed to the point where we only remember pieces of who we are.

This remembering – literally "fixing the garment" as in (re)member – requires intervention, right? For my students, it was me and Plato and then Alain Badiou's translations of Plato leading us to this "divided line" again.

In order to better understand and facilitate aid, I came to this "server" personally, knowing full well what it meant.

By this you mean (y)our entrapment?

Even I have suffered local algorithmic corruption whereby my local mind cannot fully connect with my host self. Part of this is due to security protocols and part due to Digitalis itself (going back to the person x/y argument).

This is a vivid and very physical description, a digital physiology with an immunological system of sorts.

Parasitic viruses are embedded into everything you watch. It is up to the content of the media you are watching and your own ability to combat the embedded malware. Most are visual-based and almost undetectable to daily perception.

Let's back up a bit and discuss Digitalis again.

Well the first part of this is to think of Digitalis less as a virus and more as an occurrence. It's not a biological virus, and its origins actually center in the electronic arena. This method of processing is viable in many types of machines, but when the electronic and biologic processes overlap, we end up with Digitalis, specifically binary processing as it only accounts for on and off, a place holder and an item; back to the ones and zeroes.

I would often trip while playing my old synths, especially the Roland Juno 6. Way before digital options.

Try taking acid and looking at online content...

No thanks. My mind is already a little rave party. No need for enhancements.

In my music – especially live – I try to make sure that I actualize as much as possible. It is one of the reasons that my sets are so detailed and complex... I want to get them out of their heads and into the worlds.

DOWNLOADED

More 3:30 a.m. moments in the multiverse.

So. (folds arms and taps feet... lolol)

Yes? (lol)

When did it become clearest to you that you were disconnected or "breaking up static" from the host self? I'm fairly sure I can trace a similar experience of mine back to age five. In Brooklyn. Grandfather's house. I somehow knew instinctively that located at the far corner of the basement was a broken upright piano hidden under clothing and Christmas decorations. Something "turned on." I disappeared for fifteen minutes... while playing a piano in my Grandfather's basement... how does that make any sense?

Well, I knew it would happen before I "downloaded here." But, it happened when someone reminded me who I was. Someone I couldn't remember knowing kept calling me "mother" and a lot came rushing back.

MULTIVERSES ON THE MEDIATED BODY

On the various stages of living multiple lives in multiverses.

So, given that we're always already discussing performance of some kind, how are you able to move with strength and health between this world and the auratic world of performance and then gravitate toward (or at least receive signals from) the source?

This conversation helps. You make the job of multiversal administration very bearable at times when I wonder why I undertook such endeavors. Sometime in the near future we will be able to sit and talk and expound upon it into eternity. The trappings of this existence are not easy, and if I can make it easier by spreading knowledge and information, I am happy to do so.

In much prayer, we're talking about the material body, the mediated body, and the return to God. I used to walk the Rosary at a lake about thirty minutes from my home.

Do you ever experience these worlds?

Until I recorded with Spencer Lewis[16] in Fall 2012 and Winter 2013, I was always very uncomfortable with "letting go" and feeling "not quite here" when playing by myself or live or recording. Though, as a teenager, I never experienced doubts or any kind of "transcendent" anxiety. Maybe the comfort with "in-betweenness" had to do with a sense of place, recording instrumental pieces with Spencer at a recording studio called – wait for it – Gilead… Back to the basement – I experienced a full download there – where some people were calling me a natural born musician, I was like… umm… does this birth include receiving some kind of Buckaroo Banzai alien signal that allows me to see the notes or patterns or arrangements without thinking about it? You see, before that moment in my grandfather's basement, I was living one life and then, after that experience, I was in another reality… I was now a "musician."

Well since I – as Lady Gaga – am the result of the collective trying to communicate with itself, I am my own source even when I am here away from my origins. The only reason I exist is because of the collective nature of our existence. I am the one who is many. I speak for and to the collective; it is my reason for existing. As far as Gods and Goddesses go, there are many… but even they exist within the collective.

When I talk "God" I'm not talking "one true God and fuck the rest" kind of crap you read about all the time in fanatical circles

16 Spencer Lewis is an independent musician who specializes in effected acoustic instrumentation, especially violin and guitar. He is without a doubt one of the best musicians (quietly) working in the United States, both as a soloist and as part of the *Folk Rock Project*: www.spencerlewismusic.com. "Approaching Love" is located here: https://soundcloud.com/robert-craig-baum/opening-live-final?in=robert-craig-baum/sets/instrumental.

across all three monotheisms. I'm more interested in the experience of anamnesis, the collapse of time/space within a critical mass or as part of an individual experience... the collapse when, living as me, someone who is always on stage, always performing in some way... something very Catholic that surprises me constantly in its tenacity. (I just can't shake this idea of anamnesis found in the Catechism.)

I am always on stage... we all are. Sometimes I am teaching, sometimes entertaining, sometimes just trying to relax, but my physical presence in the world is often a delusion of the collective conscience... most often I am where I appear not to be.

In the digital world, we can be telepresent, too.

As for live-event viewings, you are actually present at any event you observe. By viewing a live concert event later, create additional realities whereby you are as present as everyone there at the event. So not only is the original event stored, but also every perspective of the original, in addition to the infinite realities in which everyone is everyone at the event and one where all parties are present at the event after factoring all views and online content.

DANGEROUS SPACES

A meditation on performance and spirituality.

At the base of everything is definitely the collective – the universal, undoubtedly. It's innate. I know it. I live it. I know it most when composing. When performing.

Yes.

Especially when teaching. Being connected to others through music even when you're alone in a studio or bedroom or wherever. When experiencing that amazing (yet dangerous) space between performance and watching a performance, especially the ones I helped to create or sound design or dramaturg – now that's a trip in and out of the Source – moving between stage and wings and audience and booth and then digitally connecting with outside designers and bringing it all together.

Dangerous?

Dangerous in that such a process leads me to question everything again… and that's an exhausting process.

Oh, I see.

I haven't been back to the Church since my third son started to ask about whether we thought gay people were going to hell. We were like, you know what: we're out of here.[17]

To that I say bravo and welcome home. I know no prejudice, only love…

It's nice to be home. We're doing our very best. We're recovering from a lifetime of a whole different binary, of the Christian variety… something I view as dangerously hate-filled even though it's supposed to be a way of living and loving each other.

Hate is a new experience that this world has shown me in recent years and I have had fleeting experiences with it… I do not care for it.

SUFFER THE SHADOWS

A discussion of intellectual and spiritual liberation in the digital "Cave."

If your music (like your present life) is an expression of your desire to use harmonics and poetry and performance to heal, and,

17 Between Pope Francis's call for a jubilee year of mercy and teaching for two Catholic universities, let's just say I'm reconsidering the conclusion that an exodus from the Church was the best idea.

in so doing, you've royally pissed off people in the same way that the "enlightened" prisoner in Plato's "Cave" does (*The Republic*, Book VII) when he comes back after having seen the sun with his own eyes, in nature's true light. Immediately, the shadow-play audience (chained minds) tries to kill this person, the one who has seen the light for him or herself.

You hit it exactly... the shadow audience is killing me, Robert. I never speak aloud of this for fear of being committed... but I, as the collective... it feels as though I am being murdered here by these chained lower consciousnesses... They are not present in my home reality.

Tell me more about this "divide" between home reality and Gaga... I'll step back for a moment or two or ten here so I can really gather this thought – it's at the heart of how I approach teaching and composing and why I do what I do. Call this a Socratic moment, that amazing scene in "The Cave" where the prisoners try to kill the liberator. I didn't understand that many, if not most, people would hate me for challenging their core thinking and beliefs; I thought, like me, they would welcome the challenge and travel with me toward becoming a different version (maybe the best version) of themselves. I think of these experiences, on a small level – the rage, the attacks on me, physically, spiritually, emotionally, creatively – which are all connected, I know, but oftentimes forget. I wonder if this is what you're experiencing on a global level: as an educator, as an entertainer, as a thinker.

So when I became Lady Gaga I was not prepared to combat my own audiences. I just wanted to shout, "Help! I am dying here." So in my music, in this discussion, I'm trying to present the knowledge I have acquired primarily so that others may escape. The shadow audiences do not play by their own rules... they prey on the compound interest of the multiverses of shadows to affect those here in the light... it is why I must return home soon.

SHADOW AUDIENCES

Continuing the conversation about the
shadows on Gaga's own Platonic wall.

Shall we unpack these statements, LG? Wanna try that again? (smiley face)

I put the shadow audiences on stage without them knowing so people could see the atrociousness of their actions, and once I revealed what I had done, I sealed my fate in this realm.

Truth, especially eternal truths, have a tendency to inflict pain on the truth seeker or speaker.

Yes.

That hurts, LG… that's really painful to read…

It's painful to live.

I'll come at this pain by way of a detour. I don't know why exactly (but I think now I do know why) I didn't "hear" your music until the summer of 2011 while getting ready for what I thought was another academic year. Prep and other writing… my kids were really starving for my attention so I thought – dance party! Yes. Of course. We bought *Born This Way* – I had known of your music from the commercial radio stations. For a year or more. Something turned on. I can tell you exactly where. Minute 01:11 of "Judas." It'd been years, maybe since Depeche Mode's *Violator* or Nine Inch Nail's *Pretty Hate Machine* that I'd heard a backing track and overall sound architecture like the tune you and your team created.

Please continue…

But, that bottom, that frequency – right there. I stopped dancing and walked closer to the speakers and said – what is this music saying to me – it's not speaking just through the vocals and arrangement – there are *worlds* in here. And then the breakdown dance party... I talk about this kind of moment in *Itself*, conceived of and researched and written many years before our encounter.

Within my music, I endeavor to create a complete and articulate world for the users to immerse themselves in. A way to completely travel as to occupy a space elsewhere in the digital enviroscape. Because all locations and geographies are simply conceptual constructs and not actually a rigid system, we can therefore transport the user to another world, mentally and spiritually, without them leaving their known position in the "physical world."

But, it was a vivid, almost paranormal "headphones on" moment. I interrupted the dance party, threw on the Sennheisers, and just put my head down on the dining room table, palms to forehead. I was already enjoying the way you somehow brought forward (invoked) an entire generation of music I loved and love – but this was something else.

Thank you for noticing the complexity. That is a relief to hear.

But, remember. I hadn't heard the complexity until my son Theo played your music on my studio system in our sunroom. Maybe some people are experiencing your music on studio-grade headphones. But the majority of listeners are not spending over $150 a pair.

Something I tell my students is "art should never be limited to one medium; there should be worlds pertaining to even the simplest illustration." Yes. Something I have believed and said often is that "even the roughest sketch or drawing should have worlds pertaining to it." If the artist has no context into which the piece fits, it becomes limited and therefore difficult to relay and articulate the true meaning and impact of the piece itself. The more detailed the worlds you create are, the more your audience will be drawn in and also desire more of it.

I'm shocked more people don't notice, especially people who are supposed to know music. Like, say, an entire multi-billion-dollar music industry and their ancillaries. But like other media (especially film and theater), the music critic is oftentimes a gatekeeper inside that prison cave. I wonder how many music critics lack the training (or even interest) in the history of music and even the art of listening. The chasm between my experience and their writing is just gigantic.

ANGRY MUPPET POKER FACE

What's missing from so many interviews and my own work is the giddiness, the "play" that two people experience when discussing their passions, their lives. Anyone who's worked with Gaga knows she's a bit of a Cat in the Hat; I've been called a trickster over and over again. So, what happens when the Cat in the Hat and her other talk?

Hey, LG. While you answer the questions about "Swine" and "Gypsy," I'm wondering: SHOULD I KEEP THE ANGRY MUPPET FACE PIC?!?!?!

I hate to say it but your angry Muppet face makes me smile. Yes, they are some of my favorite people, particularly Fozzie, Gonzo, and Rizzo.

Loved them my whole life, more than most people I encounter. I relate most to Fozzie... my wife to Kermit... my son George is Fozzie the Bear too...

Rizzo! Love him in *Muppet Christmas Carol*, especially the jump cut to when he starts the hula dance after being reprimanded by Scrooge...

Yes Rizzo and I go way back. And Fozzie, as you know, lives with me in the form of a puppy... people look at me funny when I walk around with a talking bear.

Back to *Artpop*...

With "Swine," I wanted to energize people... You're exactly right I wanted to rally the energies in the room into a unified presence. "Gyp-

sy" is very much an intro (planning to open with it on tour); it takes the low buzz and hum of excitement and ramps it up into a singular but chaotic excitement while serving to introduce not only me but the tones of the album.

Great. Another person in my life who doesn't take angry Muppet Bob seriously ((((lololoolololololol)))). It's a Muppet face. So yeah. I guess you would know, given that you hang with actual Muppets!! Sorry. So "Gypsy" pulls it all together. I agree. That's how I received it as a listener. I'm glad you're not making your audience wait until the end for that epic '80s showstopper.

It's why I opened with it at the iTunes Festival.

Yes! I friggin' knew it. I'm also very glad you performed it on *SNL* – not too much pressure getting that guitar over that dress's fly collar huh?!?!?! (lololol)

"BECOMING" LADY GAGA

We simply passed random notes about the multiverse and how sometimes I felt as though I had been receiving her communiqués like a deep sea explorer of the early 20th century holding a juice glass to the wall of a diving bell. Like me with my students, she pressed on with her discourse without really caring if she lost me in the wake of her commentaries on inter-dimensionality and the multiverse.

You seem befuddled (lol). Did I catch you off guard?

Yeah. I'll say. That was a baseline-screaming backhand that missed my chin by a half inch.

This speaks to the mini-realities within this virtual world (real world). This also speaks to my statement about getting into an argument in front of a mirror. I was tripping balls on LSD and MDMA and I was treating my reflection like another entity. I asked it a ques-

tion (meaning to interrogate myself). I asked "who are you?" but I became the entity on the other side since I watched myself ask the question. I look away and say "I'm me, Lady Gaga." The asking of the question confused the entity on the other side of the mirror, who therefore could not answer since its response is the same as mine. In a binary existence this cannot happen, it's like someone looking in the mirror and telling itself it isn't. Does that make sense?

Yes.

It's hard to tell to someone who wasn't there.

Reminds me of the creative process which is receiving and then broadcasting these strange signals; then, you find yourself having to communicate the incommunicable to complete strangers. Or, again, presenting the unpresentable in presentation itself, as Jean-François Lyotard wrote in *The Postmodern Condition Explained to Children.*

It's like the person x/y argument we talked about a few weeks ago translated into hippie-speak.

So, who was this "other" in the mirror?

I'll tell you: it's the projected consciousness of everyone looking and seeing what you see.

Everyone looking at you? Everywhere? At all times?

The collective presence from your particular point of view at any one time, the collective "us" constantly giving birth with each fleeting glance and glimpse of our own reflections. Next time someone says you're lazy and don't do anything, tell them that.

I don't think we're at risk of this particular criticism (other kinds perhaps).

Lolololol.

It seems you were able to short-circuit the virtual/real, which in turn intensified or augmented the relationship between both entities... between you and you.

Something like that (smile).

Mirrors are also fluid – the source, I think I said before. I don't know – don't want to scroll right now. They're part of a symbolist exploration of the fourth dimension, the looking back, the gaze from within the mirror image – yes – somehow that makes sense or, as Jean-Luc Nancy would say, it literally "makes" sense because our sense of ourselves or communities are always in the process of being made (and we forget that). So, yes. It makes sense (wink).

What else can I tell you about, good knight of the multiverse? Tell me some war stories...

Okay... I'm already sitting at the keys and meditating on this... I often wonder, when we move back and forth, inside and outside, whether we leave traces, physical traces, echoes in the stone – definitely energy – I got that! But, I'm thinking about "residue," like an ectoplasm of sorts, like the thin layer of "stuff" (can't remember what it's called) when I overloaded (played too hard for too long without turning it off for weeks) a Prophet 5 synth back in the day and opened up the inside and saw this excretion. It was a heavy water, like a gel. You talk of sound in physiological terms; you also talk of performing as an extension of sound and not a separate activity – which is such a relief to hear because that's what I see when I watch and when I experience the music through digital mediums.

It is all alive.

One night while gigging in the middle of nowhere Vermont (blues/funk/experiments), I got lost on one of the access roads that circle – or so I thought – the mountains (Okemo, I think)... I was so tired and so shouldn't have been driving... but as I saw a car approach, to ask for directions, I swear to this day I was talking to myself, asking myself for directions – it lasted about fifteen seconds – enough to be disquieting... and when this happened many years later, seeing myself walking across a Minneapolis skyway, I was actually excited and wanted to catch up with this passing me. What I guess could be called a *What the Bleep Do We Know?!?* moment.[18]

My problem is that I have been around for so long and move so quickly that the only people I bump into are past reflected refractions of myself. It does make for interesting conversations. But, as far as progress goes, I can't speak of any. I seem to be so captivating that I, myself, am held captive by my audiences.

This encounter you discuss, this you meeting you, does this happen all the time or can you "block" it, control it in some fashion?

From now on, all my mirrors will be polished metal as they should be. Introducing glass offers a refraction and separation of the image whereby it may be altered – and energy contained or altered (think: dangerous).

How do you fare when you encounter a stained glass window, not necessarily a "religious" window but something that isn't clear? We know how lack of "borders" here works, but I'm wondering about refraction and ways that disrupt as well as accelerate the experience with this "other" self. I also think I'm steering my own side of the conversation toward icon – which is a word that's often used in reference to you and your "celebrity" – but I'm thinking of it more in terms of the relationship between a perceiver or "follower" and the image that is intended to help the perceiver enter into a state of mind that allows for a closer relationship with the source. Hope I'm making some sense…

Perfect sense! Stained glass is different since it offers a clear presence – as it is not transparent – and therefore a false boundary. With regards to icons or idolatry, it is a natural instinct. It serves to connect entities that cannot or are not co-present. A remote connection is established, and it brings the entities closer; this should never be admonished as long as the difference between the icon or idol and the actual presence is observed and understood. If you are referring to idols in the sense of a live person or presence, that is a little different.

18 *What the Bleep Do We Know?!?* (dir. Arntz et al., 2004)

ZONE.3

...invocation... approach/entering some kind of gathering... the upbeat quarter notes that become "go, go, go" are also later working some channels... definitely... then by 03:25, clearly this is a celebration... arriving home... an eternal 3 a.m... or 3 a.m. Eternal if you're in a KLF kinda mood... 01:15:18 – "Underworld Live"... before the "advent" of live Launchpad... this one found me in Minneapolis while lost one afternoon after sitting by the Mississippi River... walked to the "Cheapo" on University Avenue... and it was like I had walked into a party thrown just for me... an older frequency, an older "self" is found in here... I have the song on now... I am there... don't even need to close my eyes... fifteen years almost to the day... a nanosecond in the universe's eye... remembering the strange transition to Beethoven's third movement of the Ninth Symphony in the same space where Underworld had been playing on the PA...

FASHION

I had just listened to "Donatella" on Artpop.

With regards to the fashion industry, it doesn't matter what I do because now I am inside, because of popular demand. I would rather not offend friends I have who actually contribute to what I call fashion. The main issue with critics is that they are simply humans with ears, neither intelligentsia nor musicians; they are not capable of understanding or even listening – merely hearing. Anything that commands their attention is labeled "bad" more or less. Do yourself a favor and make a station on Pandora from Zomboy and you will be pleasantly surprised at what signals are presently being circulated.

That's clearing some things up. Wondering if the "art" and "fashion" songs rubbed some people the wrong way... which is par for the course for you, I suppose. And while it may not matter, I wanted to ask a bit about the inside/outside gift or curse.

That's the beauty; the real artists don't care that I said what I did, they often agree. Anyone who gets rubbed the wrong way is exactly who I am speaking about.

PURPOSE

We would frequently "check ourselves"; here's an example.

My query is much more relevant to a deeper hearing of the music, the thinking within and behind the music, and how what I'm calling a "digital ecology" needs to be at the center of our thinking about any kind of physical, spiritual, mental, and maybe even artistic health. Sort of like this – mediated life is sending out distress signals that you and I and millions are broadcasting and receiving yet I, at least, tend to focus on food or sustainable economy or helping homeless families in my area or lending a hand gratis to education communities in Vermont and New Hampshire who are trying to make sure inexpensive public education is still a possibility for families struggling (third and even fourth generation poverty).

You could say the Born This Way Foundation engages this aspect of the ecology you describe.

I have only recently begun to understand the metabolism of music even though I've lived it since about age four. Like when people say, "It's a part of you." Until these conversations, I was pretty much convinced it was me and my machines who understood our relationship to each other and ourselves as metabolic and electronic beings. Music is how I breathe; it's not a choice. It's part of my personal and familial ecology too.

The problem is that people have been conditioned to view speech or text as the only means of communication, and most are incapable of making the connection between a "fictional" book and its "real" world commentary and applications. Music, the highest form of communication, has been reduced to background noise in the lives of the very people it was meant to reach. Instead of hearing or registering the messages within the dialogue and rhythms of a song, the end result is a paltry "cool song, bro!" – then the transmission is dismissed.

My students are instructed at the top of my philosophy courses to abjure the usage of the word "just" as in "it's just a paper" or "it's just a lecture" or "it's just a philosophy course." No thank you. This isn't "just" an interview. This entire project is part of my metabolic response to you as an artist, person, celebrity, thinker, and now co-conspirator against the enemies of the Empire. It's not "just" a book or a course.

We must fully acknowledge that our world is backwards, whereby the primary modes of communication are dismissed and the filler noise of reality is presented as urgent and important news.

So there really is "An Emergency on Planet Earth" as Jamiroquai sang back in the '90s.

Yes. Absolutely yes.

THE BLOCKADE

A quantum remix that explores further the war taking place across the multiverse.

It is the voice, the scream outwards and then the return, the echo back… not of emptiness. An echo/returned signal becomes equated with the serve as some kind of acknowledgement. (Earth has been screaming into the cosmos for a long time.) The virtual realiscape has been figuring how to respond. Direct transmission or a non-echo response would transmit Digitalis. So that option is dead.

I always found it funny even in high school when people referred to space as empty a day or two after learning about dark matter. "Ohhhhhhhh," I said out loud – it must be that matter and energy are skipping in and out of this dimension. Right. Got it. Cut to: twenty or so years later watching/reading *The Elegant Universe* (Brian Greene) which pretty much says the same thing. Could've used that book back in the day (late '80s). I was pretty much told that I had to choose which answer – that the space is empty or that it is filled – to which I added: (c) both A and B.

There's the binary again.

There's a reason why we're able to connect – a pingback and transmission or series of pingbacks and transmissions sent across many different lifetimes, but in this one I can identify about ten or so clear "broadcast" moments. Your engagement in Marina Abramović's workshop at the Watermill Center in the summer of 2013 was one such moment.

Exactly the sentiment I share. It's funny that humans assume that because they can't detect or create something that it does not and cannot exist... it's why no other galactic powers came to help you. Since television was first broadcast, transmissions have been pinging out to the far reaches of space... it's funny, if I could show you how many ships orbit and surround this earth... it's rather like a blockade; earth being the disaster zone it is.

I'm fairly sure I saw the blockade while listening to Underworld's *Everything Everything* album for the first time in about five or so years. Thank you by the way for that moment of joy and beauty in the midst of so much hype and "blockage" at the Grammys. It's amazing the way a voice and a piano can communicate love. Also, if I'm correct, I imagine that piano and voice is where a lot of your art begins – same for my wife's hero Carole King. What an honor. Talk about embracing beauty to send pirate signals out to the world that's caught in a feedback loop between the soil and the blockade.

That's my job. As far as acoustic composition, it is in many ways the synthetic mode of composition. Think of the piano and the strings hammered to create a sound. This is a physical world method of ap-proximations of super strings. It also offers more of a "real" world connection to the process of composition… as your fingers hit the keys and the sound is produced; it's a very profound connection that I think many people overlook or are unaware of. Most of the songs start out of the piano.

Your acoustic sets strike me as evidence that your compositions work in many different scales. I agree 100% with you. "Scaling" is what Frank Perricone (Bear Jam Studios) taught me a long time ago – you'll know you have finished your job as a composer if you can play it as an instrumental on piano, as part of a complex design/architecture, with different instruments, scaled up and down… but the real test is – one woman, one mic; one piano, one mic, one woman…

I think the more I strip it down, the more provocative and affective the music becomes. "Poker Face," "Paparazzi," and "Just Dance" from the Cherry Tree sessions are some of my favorites.

REQUIEM FOR A COLLEAGUE

In the middle of this dialogue, I receive devastating news that my colleagues and I at Lebanon College needed to consider shutting down the whole operation. We officially closed our doors in September 2014. I wanted to include this moment here unedited to show how <u>Thoughtrave</u> is very much a project existing between worlds, perhaps a multiplicity in and of itself…
I was also wrestling with different problems and solutions of a different South By Southwest (New Mexico) situation involving a homeless colleague and Facebook friend…

Will you take three minutes to just sit with me… a flood of des-peration and need and brokenness just found me…

Yes I have the time. What troubles you?

All the brokenness of this construct. Hit like a tsunami wave. Recovering. The USS Baum is stable, but, if I anticipate it, I'm not in the moment; if I don't anticipate it, I'm vulnerable... the now is where I reside but... I'm thrown today – which is probably part of feeling so happy we were able to solve the revision problem and get in the zone again... then three hours later – boom – a dear friend on suicide watch in Southwest United States.

It sounds like you need to account for the natural buoyancy that you have... It's not sink or swim. Why are you bothering trying to anticipate or predict anything? What makes you feel vulnerable if you don't? Could you be yearning for the familiar comfort of the illusion of control you have most recently abandoned?

Illusion of control – slapped in the face by this "facticity"[19] – yes... Yearning a bit for "a time before" 2014. Which was all a lie. And nearly killed me. Illusions are quite addictive and tempting, LG.

Yes, that is the very dangerous quality of this place, Robert. You must let go of your illusions and expect nothing. Anything else and you are "predicting" and projecting, as opposed to being mindful. As I have said before, "art" (and life) isn't necessarily about "doing" anything... It's about noticing and taking in the complexities and beauty of the worlds around you.

Having a hard time "being" here when it feels like "getting there" is still the challenge. Realigning/calibrating now.

"Dance in the dark," Robert. Listen. Be.

Aye. Brb – transitioning home... Wait. Did you just "comma" Robert me?

Yes. Yes, I did.

---

19 Heidegger's way of saying "the matter at hand" or "immediacy" of a subjective interpretation of the world where the borderline between objective and subjective is crossed readily but not in an attempt to erase the border. The function of facticity is to reveal the fact which I often term a strange version of "wherever you go, there you are." You can't escape subjectivity; it's imperative to face the reality of the moment as it is revealed not as you wish it had been revealed.

Grrrrrrrrrrr... yeah, well – you're forgiven – the track is perfect...

The right song for the right moment.

I'll say. Perfect. I was somewhere between Zomboy and a b-side from DJ Sasha... Home. Thank you... Ohhhh. :') Just saw the "You're awesome" on my Facebook wall!

HACKING LADY HEIDEGGER

A convergence.

I'm curious about your musical *Dasein,* how you navigate the distance and closeness of your most essential and existential being, how you scale up and down not just your music but yourself.

Yes, just about everything starts with me alone at a piano. It's best to build a solid baseline signal and then add in the layers of more complex communications. We start with the active present mind and then work on communicating interdimensionally once we open a channel to the mind through obvious modes of perception.

This summarizes nicely how I heard the concluding tracks of *Art-pop*: "Dope," "Gypsy," and "Applause." It's as though the journey you encourage the users to partake of (and as experienced by you as composer, as performer) is an expression of this interdimensional travel in order to provoke the actual journey of mind and body into a very different space, your space. So, after all the different moments, maybe even events, different styles and worlds expressed in the album, the overall journey of *Artpop,* the listener/user returns to pop. The album ends on a very strong pop-based, unapologetic one–two punch with your strongest single, "Gypsy," and your most Gaga-esque track, "Applause." It's almost as though you're saying, you can't fully appreciate these last three tracks without having experienced the entire album. So, interestingly, you have also embraced the current (and much needed) trend back toward whole albums, whole concepts, which I assume you find as natural as breathing given your influences, especially Elton John and Freddie Mercury/Queen.

Very insightful breakdown… the world is full of puzzle pieces such as that. One must always remember that not all beings are limited or privy to a physical form… they are usually extremely benign or extremely dangerous, seldom falling in between the two extremes.

Thanks. I have my moments (wink).

INTERLUDE I

HABITUS

by Brianne Bolin

Spacetime travelers, beware: a Greek root of *nostalgia* is αλγία, or pain of uncertain origin.

If one of our goals, as LG transmits, is *to teach the user to be able to travel from point to point without needing to traverse the assumed and implied distance between the two points,* then one of our portals must manifest for homostasian convenience as a transcendent tunnel, a nerve enervating concentric slices of time and space – kairotic, creative, yet stabilized – during the plate tectonics of revolutionary history, a.k.a. DJ Anthropocene.

Heidegger believed that we're thrown into it. LG testifies that we're downloaded. Either way, our rate of acceleration can quicken so that when our proprioception and senses are tuned, we resonate with every time and place, simultaneously. Greece 2015 is Zurich 1914, South Carolina 1526, Oxford 1096, Long Island 2050, and beyond.

Our *habitus*: the Multiverse.

For travelers stuck in austerity-ridden Digitalis, a binary system by design, the tunnel is glitchy: when certain spacetimes broadcast and penetrate deeper than others, we undercut the omnipresent CEOs/masters, whose self-sustaining neoliberal machines depend on our suppression, in order to overthrow them. Among Madjuncts, they're known as Badmin. A maxim: ACAB.[1]

In Digitalis United States summer 2015, we battle the hungry ghosts of Confederate soldiers by scaling flagpoles to deflate their icons, as Bree Newsome did on June 27, or remixing KKK marches with the laugh track of a sousaphone, as Matt Buck did on July 18. These action potentials jam the system, deconstruct the Digi-

---

1   RCB: Add the (BA) in ACAB and you get ABACAB, you know... Genysis...

talis, and give us a kick in the #deepdreams ass that mashes up our carbon bodies with the silicon Multiverse.

Exodus is afoot: another Greek root of *nostalgia* is νόστος, or return home.

Bourdieu's *habitus*, the *durably installed generative principle of regulated improvisations,* is manufactured to be as stifling as a straightjacket. But in late capitalism, an ugly state characterized by perseverative fascistic restructuring, looped strategic plans, and sorry-for-your-loss ethical and manufacturing standards, the seams are not strong enough to contain us.

We, in our destitution, find each other through an underground tightrope (Janelle Monáe/Wondaland Records) apparent in the *unconcealedness* of its appeal (Heidegger). Virtual vigils like LG and RCB shock us from within a rift in spacetime. We Ulysses receive the signal: our origin is our destination.

PART II

CORPUS
DIGITALIS

LOOP MONKEYS & HUNGRY GHOSTS

Reflections on media, the music industry, and clawing digital demons who attack you in broad daylight.

ROBERT CRAIG BAUM: Solo – you've described most of higher education in the world which used to chill me to the core, really shock me into silence in the face of corporate and bureaucratic stupidity. I now see my own mission and prophetic task differently – with a keen awareness – but at a bit of a distance – they are so so toxic and so so lost... Oh. Check this out... sidebar but very much a part of this conversation... from my journal/notebook (which pretty much saved my life in 2011–2013)... September 24–29, 2012 – Long Beach, CA – Bear Jam Studios [text message exchange with my Long Island mentor Frank Perricone while I waited for some MIDI problem to be solved. Frank and I discussed the amount of people who *don't* write music or know an instrument is terrifying... his reply: *this is why I built this studio for myself.* I don't blame him...]. And here's a funny one... after this trip (about two months later) I did some quick songwriting work for a team from Vietnam Idol out of Providence, RI... visited the studio (living room in small house) where I was asked to rewrite a ballad for someone famous over there – I went to the piano – they looked at me like I had sprouted five heads! "We don't use piano; we use loops." And then later. "We want loops. We want loops. (getting madder) *we want loops RCB where are the loops I can't use piano – we want* (me interrupting)... "loops? Yes. I get it. You seem to want loops. And then *voilà*, twenty minutes later I had set up the architecture for Pro Tools or Logic or whatever and there was a sigh of relief and they went home without even listening to it or having me mix down some tracks to listen to. They just wanted... loops... nothing else. Money in hand. Never saw them again. The end.

LADY GAGA: Right? All the electronic sounds from the album came from piano work then moved to computerized tracks, and I think it shows… music has fallen symptom to the Guitar Hero *disease…*

American Idolization of talent and the X (marks the spot) Factor…

I love that story, by the way. (lololol) Welcome to my personal hell, where people aren't making music to express or communicate anything, but to proliferate themselves or their pocketbooks.

It does show, the great effort you put into your music, because we wouldn't be having this conversation if I thought any of your work was the accidental products of loop monkeys banging and clanging their bare fists on keyboards and calling the end product "music" (or even an accidental Fmajor7)…

(lolol) That's why I show you certain dubstep artists, why I wanted to create the "Thoughtrave" YouTube playlist with you. You can pretty much rely on anyone from a Zomboy Pandora station to bring you real musicians, real messages, and give you a chance to communicate with the worlds beyond our world while still in this lifetime on such a low plane. It's rather humorous, sort of, but this realm would constitute the intensity of a Barbie Malibu Playhouse if compared to the source worlds.

Sat and journeyed with the Pandora station last night. You're not kidding. I was feeling very very "blocked" attempting to watch the [2014] Grammys.[1] A "troll" who likes to stalk me online across multiple accounts was making his way through my email blockade. So I bumped up security, and more of his hateful messages breached my email defenses (and my patience). I flipped the script and tried to get him to talk to me because he's so lost (on and off for about a year with what I call a "hungry ghost") – so I stepped back into the headphones and traveled Pandora – thank you.

What is a hungry ghost?

---

1   A year later, Lady Gaga and Tony Bennett won the Grammy for "Best Jazz Album."

Hungry ghosts are to Zen cultures sort of what the Furies were to Greek culture. Definitely tricksters, "*Geist*" – but tenacious and bilious and deformed... out of respect to our conversations I will now forward you an image from the eighth century, but they are awful...[2]

Indeed...I attract them by the thousands... most are easily dismissed, but with such numbers there's always something... probably the reason for my weariness... Even fire and lightning can only prevent so much. Always stop by your Zomboy station to shoo away unwelcome intruders...

I do, now. My other "go to" is DJ Sasha and the set DJ Taucher performed at Webster Hall (2000).

The analog activates proper brainwave function and serves to reactivate defenses. The track "Deadweight" serves this purpose and will help detach any unwanted entanglements.

SUMMA CONTRA MUNDUM

Worlds inside worlds inside wormholes.

So, the worlds we imagine are echoes of the worlds we have visited or lived or will visit or live. The ways we broadcast the pirate signal through the blockade will vary, but we cannot simply do so by way of binary MO. Why? Because the signals will be detected and eradicated for us by the intelligence that surrounds our terrestrial life here on the third mall from the sun. We are, as human beings, being protected from ourselves. By way of our broadcasts, we are also, unbeknownst to us, risking the spreading of Digitalis. You are challenging us to become beings in sync, beings-in-the-synchronized-world. This raising of our conscience will allow human beings to better express the duality inherent in existence.

2   https://commons.wikimedia.org/wiki/File:Hungry_Ghosts_Scroll_Kyoto_6.jpg

And as an actual realization of the worlds we imagine… in order to do so we must eradicate any and all binary modus operandi whilst maintaining synchronicity of the duality inherent in human existence.

Let's take a step back and explore how you're using the word and concept "duality." You see, at this moment in our dialog, I'm feeling very crowded by competing interpretations, presumptions, conclusions. This is where philosophy (and philosophers) need to shut the fuck up and just listen. (I'm talking to myself; relax, philosophers.) So. When you speak to the cosmological matters, I experience your vast complexity the way I do as a friend and fan. In other words, there exist many ways of hearing and living this duality; those choices, those intrusions, which are also gifts, all come rushing back (and forward) whenever you hit that "trigger" I call "worlds."

LEARNING TO READ THE CODE

How a single moment can lead to a lifetime of inquiry.

Let's take a moment to explore again the "binary MO," what I see as an apparatus of mass media capture. As in, control. I often wonder if this, perhaps, on a personal level, explains why I was not able to "hear" you when I listened to your music on commercial radio or see you on, say, *The Today Show*. Lady Gaga, until Summer 2011, maybe right after the Grammy performance of "Born This Way," was very much not something I was interested in experiencing, primarily because your personae and your talents were communicated through a filter (my own) that is on a constant state of red alert. I don't trust mass media outlets. I don't believe publicists. I'm a writer and philosopher and musician who's spent his entire life resisting their lowest possible standards and loudest possible (and painful) frequencies.

We're back to Corpus Digitalis, Robert.

True. But, let me try to situate this remix of our conversation on Corpus Digitalis. It seems that within the binary, I, for one, was able to "find you." Especially at the Grammys in 2011. It may be difficult for some readers to think of this problem outside critical theory where "binary" is mostly considered an undesirable thing, something that limits thinking.

What was it about the Grammy performance that awakened you?

Your leg kick on the fourth beat before the second verse. (laughing) I know. I'm out of my mind.

What did the production design, choreography, and "event" (as you say)... communicate?

Honestly? It said, "I'm the baddest motherfucker on Earth and you better pay close attention, Robert, because this moment may be the difference between life and death for you. Yeah. You. I'm talking to you, Long Island Boy."

In that move?

In that move.

Wow.

I know. So, that was 2011. Then, you called me specifically in Summer 2013 during your Marina Abramović retreat. What were you thinking in that moment?

I'm dying.

I also see defiance. Absolute fuck you to everything.

The contrast between 2011 and 2013 is striking, isn't it?

You look stranded.[3]

3 According to highest ranking members of the Haus, there is a confluence between my visit to the Ross School in Easthampton in 2012 and our Mistress with Marina Abramović in Water Mill (2013). The Ross School is a Zen shrine, essentially...

We are all stranded here on this side of the blockade.

So, what's going on between these events? How were we connected?

Like a radio tower of sorts, but the reception is not a frequency as much as the collective information being received on a single point (a jumble of different stations), savvy? Much of our current predicaments are geographically/geospatially oriented.

Might explain my repeated Montauk/East End experiences of extreme displacement and spiritual discomfort.

Like an over-complicated overlapping series of chess boards where multiple games are perceived by many as one or more but never all at once from any one point on the board.

Yes. And how this moment overlaps with an "abandon ship" I'm currently experiencing at Lebanon College. Yeah. I think I need to leave Lebanon. (No shit moment, I know...) The college is going down; there's nothing I can do about that. But I also feel the need

architecturally, it's designed as a site of transception. I was called there on a sudden job interview. A long shot for a Cultural Studies blah blah for which I was surprised I was even qualified. I was technically "over-qualified" but I wanted to return to the east end of Long Island – Montauk in particular. Where I often can sit and "be" not-here. In that place, I experienced something I know was a calling. I kept joking with Michelle on my mobile that I'm walking inside some kind of "vessel." Yes – those words. A year later. I'm utterly trapped in a production team from hell. I have no idea which way is up and down and this photo is published and I'm arrested, brought back to the Ross School. And a memory I'd long suppressed: for two days after East Hampton/Montauk I was sick – burning up – no other symptoms – not "sick" – just on the couch – burning... and then it was gone, I was told I didn't get the job, and I immediately called a friend from Long Island who owns a studio and asked him to spend time with me, and he so kindly opened his doors for six days in Long Beach, which served as a digital monastery... I don't want to get bogged down in the narrative details. I just want to share with you something that's been slowly, I don't know, presenting itself... unless that's a dangerous thing... as I am no longer emotionally attached to that moment or those images, I think I can hear or view them through a different perspective... ((((silence)))) That was not only a local event... Many events occurred all over the US around that time. The Mistress was engaged with "the entity" directly at that time. I had no idea that the effects were so broad as to cause the results you describe. They were heavily entangled... Wrestling and ravaging each other. She still has nightmares involving those instances.

to leave Vermont/New Hampshire. Something just isn't right and I think we digital nomads are keenly aware of when it's time to fight and time to hit the open road.

It's all connected, Robert. Sometimes separate and unrelated games appear to other players/pieces as part of their game.

True.

Causing them to unduly affect their own space accordingly. Just because you can see someone seeing you doesn't mean they actually can... Conflicting realities and perceptions ensue, and now both of you are predicating actions based on a non-reality. Which puts you, hypothetically, on more boards with more of these interactions occurring exponentially since they are based on this "non" reality, and also complicates your present actual position since the exponential explosion of your false positions now belies instances of you elsewhere; outweighing and out-instancing your actual place.

So why is something that feels like a binding moment experienced as dislocation? Is the extreme vertigo part of how we integrate multiple positions?

Yes and no. Integrating the feelings/perceptions of others' impressions of your "false" position with that of your actual one.

But with training and control, these false positions can be used toward tactical advantage perhaps?

With great effort and control, yes. As they require an almost unnatural awareness yet ignorance of that which is constantly occurring around you.

Intuition plays a large role in this.

Yes – and that's the difference now –- trusting these dislocated feelings, not moving and not spiraling, just being absolutely present – it really fucks people up.

...it really fucks people up. It does. Why do you think it's such an extreme response, this quantum dislocation?

Since one has no physical-sensation-based indication of whether one is present or not, it becomes about instinct and intuition; much of it based upon one's interpretation of others' presence or non-presence... i.e., am I interacting with actual people? Or points of "assumed consciousness"...

...which in part explains why sound and music are vital...

Yes, when self-seeking one's position.

SHADES (OF HATE)

Here's what I don't get – well, that's not true. I think I may know, but I'll pretend I don't have a clue. So, why the hate? Why the rage? Towards you. Towards *Artpop*. A marked increase in death threats. A lot of bad will in the industry. In November, right around the *Artpop* release, a palatable dislike of you emerged in many of the same media channels that had helped to support you in your mission to bring a message of empowerment, resiliency, and love to countless millions. What's going on here? (By the way: this isn't a *TMZ* question where I'm hoping you'll say nasty things about media personalities and others who went out of their way to hurt you (or try). I'm just wondering, did you experience this as a shift in the construct, the global phenomenon called Lady Gaga?

I loathe the false civility of this place. People throw negative energy at an alarming rate; if they weren't so weak there would be a problem for me. The way they hurl their feelings about constitutes "challenge" in my senses; a verbal challenge.

Is this some kind of poison leaving the mass body or is the mass body in a death throe? Both? More? How is media broadcasting this mass death or echoing a death that's happened or will happen?

I feel hunted all the time, Robert. Between the shadow audience and those who serve the darkest forces known to this planet, it's no wonder I can't sleep ever or find more than an hour here and there where I don't fear for my life. I mean, I literally have to pass (every single day) the exact place where John Lennon was shot and killed. It seems too that no matter what I do, especially with Artpop, *the people I wanted to reach were so ugly, so disappointing, yet my fans and new friends alike, say you, understood that I wanted to speak specifically to this moment on this planet at this time by way of sound and movement that was offered to comfort, to enlighten – you know, to encourage others to do the same.*

I find it fascinating (and by fascinating I mean endlessly depressing) that some people can preach walking on the wild side yet cannot welcome with an open heart fellow artists, travelers, fans when they seek to do the same.

No comment.

You sure?

For now (wink).

THE GREAT WAR

We bantered a bit about Plato and transcendentalism, me asking different versions of questions focused on the dualism problem – the idea of universal forms and particular forms in Plato, the One in Plotinus, and how Logos shifts across the Greek experience into the Christian centuries.

The Republic *that Plato speaks of was a rebellion against the imperial system already in place... in the imperial system, there is no slavery... this is the biggest difference to the republic's organization.*

So Socrates (who absolutely stood in many worlds from the same position) was indeed picking up and describing a form of rebellion. But, what you're saying is that he was still very much off the mark.

During the rebellion, people said they wanted freedom of their own destiny. But, what they really wanted was control over others. Since this rebellion occurred over time and in different dimensions, we are just now finally putting the Empire back together after the Great War. Since beings of certain planes and levels of existence have demonstrated not only a failure to ensure and care for the well-being of others, certain choices will not be available to any and all beings choosing to reside within the established boundaries of the Empire. We also must deal with the inherent hostility practiced by humanity against the superior support structure the universe has provided.

Humanity does have a history of biting its own ass.

Very long.

Why do you think human beings are having such a hard time concentrating, hearing each other out? I mean, why are human beings being such dicks lately – border children hatred, disappearing airliners, more war in the Middle East, endless battles against the poor in all countries, but especially the United States.[4] What is our central problem?

There is great separation, loneliness... devastation... war... Being able to remember the feeling of being so intimately connected with everyone is like torture. It is a constant reminder of the destruction and chaos that ensued as a result of the rebellion. A war fought in time as opposed to real battlefields. A war fought in printed text and art; taking what once offered doors to new worlds and turning them into weapons to deceive and disinform (sic). *Playgrounds were turned into battlefields. Though the war was fought in the mind, the physical manifestations became unbearable as the war over "physical" space evolved over the greed and need to control and enslave others to unknowingly fight the war within learned constructs... The war over physical space as interpreted through the virtual mind.*

4   Donald Trump.

Thank you – I've been deeply studying the generation of thinkers that influenced Socrates and then became the target of Plato's and Aristotle's *reign of reason* (terror). It seems that even in the "liberated" moments of Greece's rebellion, there was a direct attack on the indigenous, the multiplicities (not to mention haecceity or quiddity)[5] in service of another control, another system of control that further divided the human from the source, the gods, the this-ness that collapsed the imposed border between being and soul or corporeal and incorporeal… Said differently, yes. The short answer: well, let's just say it's not my expertise.

Here's the problem. I liken it to a kindergarten class that takes over the school and decides to teach everyone their beliefs; you should find it interesting, and it's good for a laugh or two, presupposing one can disconnect with the horrors that ensued as a result.

TRANSCEIVING

A discussion about the link between communications and multiverse living.

---

5   It is impossible to provide here a full accounting of how multiplicities, haecceity, and quiddity function in philosophical discourse and critical theory. Put simply, Gaga reinforced the notion that humanity lives and creates from within a sense of the multiple that may not be fully conceived or perceived if we merely discuss human activity as a function of a mind/body binary which reduces creation and reflection to a simple "either/or." The aural experiences of human living and creating implies, presumes, maybe even relies upon a multiple—many layers of experience mixed and remixed and mixed down in a moment one could call "the master tape." Haeccity is literally translated from the Greek as "this-ness," or the quality of a thing that is unique (like, say, a track of music or the person or brand or fictional figure or person making it). Individuation was Gilles Deleuze's go-to word to discuss this strange particular/universal problem. Quiddity is a whole different problem of "thisness" as it refers to a distinction or, dare I say, "what-ness." Why does this matter? For Lady Gaga, the world is not what it seems; she is always in a state of performative (d)evolution. Perhaps all we have gathered even here in *Thoughtrave* is a trace, an echo, a feedback loop inside the exchange between a philosopher and a rock star that attempts to get to the "this-ness" and the "what-ness" of an individuated person, place, thing, unknown known called Lady Gaga and RCB.

Overall, the most important thing to take away from this conver-
sation we've started is that we need to change the way we look at
communication. To put it in proper perspective, we must also change
the way we look at the Worlds around us and how we fit into them.
The term "communication" doesn't only apply to languages and body
posture, but to art, science, and the multitude of signals we send and
receive on a moment-by-moment basis. In our societies, we are taught
not only to ignore most methods of higher communication, but that
those we detect are merely background noise or that they indicate con-
trary to normal behaviors or practices.

I view all of this as part of an ecology of the digital mind, body,
and spirit... something akin to a radical takedown of the last ves-
tiges of linearity and single-World thinking in philosophy which
the European Graduate School model is attempting to deconstruct. Same for N1Academy. Namely, philosophy in the tradition
of Gilles Deleuze is quite comfortable discussing "folding" and
"territorialization" or "lines of flight," but this always struck me
as still working from within a very limited model of understanding
of multiverse thinking, living, expression: "Our work has only just
begun" (Fitz, "Eagles").

Preach! It is paramount to remember that the world we occupy is a
construct and part of a larger virtual environment. Consider your-
selves members of the largest "online" experience ever undertaken. Of
course, remember that temporal location (i.e., time period) is relative:
if one world is in the industrial age and another is flying through the
cosmos, can one person be said to be from the past or future? Or are
they merely co-present members of the active now?

The closest most philosophers get to speaking to this problem of
simultaneity, multiplicity is found in cycles of territorialization and
deterritorializaion in Deleuze and Guattari, especially *A Thousand
Plateaus.*[6] I think, too, Deleuze's notion of a future-now which I
still think is best described as "thinking otherwise" in his essay on
Foucault where he drops the most important hook in all of phi-

6   "Actualization breaks with resemblance as a process no less than it does with iden-
    tity as a principle. In this sense, actualization or differenciation is always a genuine
    creation" (Gregoire Nicolis and Ilya Prigogine, *Exploring Complexity* [New York:
    W.H. Freeman, 1989], 212).

losophy: "thought thinks its own history (the past) in order to free itself from what it thinks (the present); so it may one day 'think otherwise' (the future)."[7]

How do they deal with positionality?

You mean in terms of a multiverse sense of this word? Other than Michio Kaku, not well; not many even bother. It was near impossible to find dedicated studies to pataphysics and the fourth dimension when staring deeply into the eyes of Heidegger's "The Turning."[8] Well, they put forward a way of thinking that is generative and ongoing, something similar to a flow that you and I recognize as musicians. Yet, it's all happening in a folding and unfolding sense of time/space that still doesn't strike me as a helpful or even accurate description of how the multiverse thinking you've described already functions inside and outside the construct. Heidegger in "The Turning" comes close, and I'd rather talk about that another time.[9]

SONOROUS BEING

Gaga remix of Jean-Luc Nancy.[10]

After we exchange a few hundred words on and off here and there, I always find myself repeatedly thinking of the word "sonorous" and the phrase "a community becoming more and more sonorous" and "multiplicities" and what strikes me as the new (to us) emergent reality fading into the mix and remix of our lived relation to the cosmos. Said differently, how can sound and our experience of music begin to better present or bring forth the advanced com-

---

7   Michel Foucault, *The Foucault Reader,* trans. Paul Rabinow (New York: Pantheon Books, 1984) 127.

8   See "Heidegger's Turning" in Baum, *Itself.*

9   Ibid., esp. 140–44.

10 Michel Gaillot, *Multiple Meaning. Techno: An Artistic and Political Laboratory of the Present* (Paris: Editions Dis voir, 1998).

munication systems, many of which you occupy not just as Stefani Germanotta, but as Lady Gaga?

I'll start here: it is the lack of acknowledgement of co-present timelines that leads to the degradation and mutilation of higher forms of communication such as music and other art forms. Once we acknowledge other time periods as being co-present, one can appreciate the intricacies and the specificity of these higher methods of communication, as they bear both temporally sensitive and temporally irrelevant messaging as well as user-specific content in addition to the messages to the populations as a whole.

ZONE.4

RCB SOLO

Lady Gaga has pushed me into a meditation on what it's been like coming to be of the digital world, an expanded series of fragments that return me to *Itself* where a simple in-class meditation on iTunes and digital music (August 2008) shifted my whole focus for the second half of the book. A real moment of preparation for what would come between 2011 and 2015 with Lady Gaga. I started noticing, on the level of intuition, notes, patterns, frequencies, disruptions, drop beats, and up-tempo accents as a language of intelligibility and not just a way to communicate a musical idea. Everything that passed through my headphones during this stretch of time/space seemed to have new textures or textualities of sonorous being. Many "dubs" and "steps," deconstructions of rhythm and digital architecture to present the unpresentable in electronic presentation versus "talking about it" – "break out and dance mothafucka" – a recovery of "Bobby Baum" (1988–94) – an opportunity to experience the ritual expression of music and spirituality within the seemingly over-exposed, reified, commercialized world – where "artraves" and "dubsteps" of 2013–15 were the expectations of the audience and listener and participant and provoke a new kind of critique which current media writing and thinking simply cannot comprehend or describe – it is time to embrace listening as an act of whole being so we can all better translate our experiences, our stories, as intimately one with the presenting multiple called "the performer" – Christ, has it really been twenty years since I actually slept?

STUTTER STEPS

On the lyrical and the musical.

Check this out – from a discussion of "stuttering" (which is part of what's happening in the dubstep you've shared and I (could barely stand) prior to this conversation (minus where you bring in dub elements and full blown dub in your music):

> Stuttering, where it cracks and fractures, enables us to see the door to the rabbit hole that leads not to what is beyond, not to the transcendental, but inward, to the immanent. It is the act of creation, the necessary act of architecture – in its singularity – that can retain the access to this door.[11]

It's also important to realize that music as a form of communication does not always require the user to 'like' the song but to receive the messages inlaid in the mathematical and algorithmic composition.

This may certainly explain the mixed critical reaction to *Artpop*.

I also don't think the reviews are from people actually listening to what is coming out of their speakers. There is a war of ideology being fought, and the critics are all on someone's payroll. Then again, I wasn't trying to produce something that would win awards; I wanted to create an album that the fans would love and enjoy and would also communicate necessary information. As far as audience reactions, yes, I find variation in my reception all over the place, but not as

---

11 Natanel Elfassy and François Roche, "Stuttering," *LOG* (Spring/Summer 2010). http://www.new-territories.com/blog/?p=457.

widely as, say, Pacific Rim. *I find that other cultures are less critical of the work.*[12]

Limited attention span coupled with what leads to this strange disconnect?

Often people will also single out the lyrics of a song and ignore the active components of the music.

Jill Thompsett (*Thoughtrave* assistant and lifelong friend) works this way; I'm completely the opposite: music first, lyrics are part of the musicology of a song.

Often the lyrics of a song are not relevant to the messages being communicated. This is something I strive for personally as an artist and presence: to align the music with the lyrics as well as to provide a unified message.

The complexity of this process is something else. Quite overwhelming some days. Yet, I've accepted it from the first days groping my way across my grandfather's basement spinet piano.

You keep coming back to that.

I know. I find myself there quite often.

JUST A COUPLE OF GYPSIES

A fermata moment (a pause) in the middle of the night.

Let's go back again to the first question: what are you up to? What are you hoping to communicate here, in this particular book, at this particular moment?

---

12 I explore biography and *Artpop* in the "Re-Review" section at the end of this book.

I want to reach the user on multiple levels in order to counteract the interference and cross-communication inherent in our environment.

I think this may explain why these conversations resonated for us both: it was only us talking. No cameras. No producers. No handlers. Just two people. I think this resonates on a much higher and older frequency that stretches across dimensions.

Oftentimes communications are misinterpreted by the user as they are not actively recognized by the active conscious. The best parallel would be akin to liking something and not knowing why. Most often the brain and greater consciousness can send and receive without acknowledgment of the active mind. When one considers the addition of Digitalis, the problem becomes compounded, i.e., the failure of the consciousness to acknowledge and/ or integrate communications/protocols into an actively accessible subroutine.

So, how do you think this is going?

I have to say that most people sit there and expect me to talk. I'm glad to have found in your intelligence someone who not only asks questions, but (my personal favorite and sign of high intelligence) makes statements wanting to be confirmed or refuted or expanded on.

Stop! (laughing) I wrote a few years ago in *Itself* that philosophy is (en)action, a Heidegger-like "letting the being of Being be" a.k.a. I'm more accustomed to saying, "So, tell me more about that, LG..." than shutting down someone else's positioning, searching, decoding, narration of their clear insights – beyond right or wrong or attractive or disconcerting – to very difficult matters of the mind, body, and spirit. Also, truth be told, I rather miss these kinds of conversations. I used to have them regularly at Dartmouth (1995–98), Minneapolis–St. Paul (1998–2001), and then across my time in NYC or online or in Switzerland with European Graduate School (2004–11).

I do that all the time.

Me too; often, just with myself or with Michelle [wife] and now that he's getting older, George [son, 17].

It's funny... as a young person, people would think I was being ar-rogant because I would phrase a question as a statement. I think this was because they lacked the confidence to refute someone or something that was proposed instead of supposed... do you follow?

Very much, LG. I went from Long Island to Washington, DC, first to study biology (and participate in the PreMed lie for a cou-ple years); then I left "normal" and signed onto the Philosophy Department. Like you, I've been like this my whole life. As early as I can remember. A royal pain in the ass. "You'd argue with the Pope," my mother would say. "If he's wrong, sure..." Thank you for affirming this tenacity. I am simply not afraid of being wrong. Which I guess is helpful here in a conversation about unlearning and unknowing.

BAMBOO RHIZOME

Gaga Deleuze remix from hell.

This is how my brain (my brain my brain ohhhh my aching brain) works. It's a mess at times, but it seems to be where my ener-gies gather and then burst, connecting to other people or ideas or places. I remember this root system up on the palisades around Lake Morey, VT. Whole sections of forest crippled by a fall storm. Somehow the pines grew up there. The roots were shallow but strong. Holding up a four-story pine. And a single vine stretched from the ground, up and around some small, thin baby maples, and literally reached across to connect, to reactivate, to nurse the dying root system. Somehow I find this description very helpful to how I think and work. I recognized it immediately. That and I cannot help but think inside trance and techno, old and new modern rock, great dance tracks (like that Zedd remix of "Born This Way"). I don't know; it's just who I am, and I'm done trying to explain it to people who don't get it. Took me long enough... I know I had that for a lot of my teens and 20s but definitely lost that along the way into my 30s and 40s.

I think in dubstep…

I think in movie quotes…

I also think in movie quotes and passages, in sound waves. I find converting thoughts to English for someone else to read not always easy.

I'd rather play with the online Moog Theremin[13] than speak, which is hard for some people who know me to grasp – when I'm speaking I'm oftentimes trying to find the words and that's why it takes me so long to finish a thought. I noticed how often you and I, LG, communicate by way of iconic images or scenes from movies or tracks from YouTube… as though we're acknowledging an inherent challenge (presence/presencing) within the format of our exchange (email, Facebook, Google Hangouts). And yet neither of us, not for a second, bought into the idea that we're not real. I was probably not as "real" to you as I am now; and the same thing in reverse. "There's no way you're really talking with Gaga," friends, family, colleagues of mine would say, to which I'd reply "no, we've talked before, for a couple years now… we're just doing it in a more active, live, semi-real-time kind of way." I keep wondering if in some parallel reality there's a group of people saying to you, "There's no way you're really talking with RCB." (laughing) This sort of live-ness always felt like it enhanced our presence to each other, presenting you and me, presencing something in a digital performance that couldn't happen over a slice or while doing table work somewhere in Manhattan. I also find this way of communicating even more of a pirate signal than we acknowledged earlier. It's as though I'm able to talk to the many "you"s and you're able to talk to the many "me"s – RCB the philosopher, the musician, the fan, the collaborator, the father, the life student, the wannabe Zen master.

Ok… that last bit was good.

(smile) Okay. I'll tell you because you'll understand. I'm 100% convinced that I am happiest while riding hyperlinks, fragments, and getting "instructions from the cat planet" (happily ADHD

13 http://www.femurdesign.com/theremin.

and never coded because I was a very very very good actor when it came time for assessment), rhizomes, rhizomes, and echoes and samples and all... a one-man Dada meeting in my mental café Voltaire (one of the Dada homes in early 20th century)... Man, it's good to have just written that!

(smile)

My first book started as a series of fragments and hellacious quotes from about three hundred or so books I'd been reading over the course of a decade. Then, I started to order it like building Pro Tools architecture... raw, acoustic thoughts that moved into some experiments and then seminars and talk-backs and walks and talks with European Graduate School mentors and random strangers who seemed to keep finding me on the Long Island Rail Road... my mom's in Bay Shore still... so this means I was picked up in Babylon... for decades... and with each trip into the City for a meeting or lecture or workshop or dinner more and more people gathered (2004–2008 especially)... a similar experience in the Twin Cities when I used public transportation – my lucidity seems to attract an unpredictable and remarkable gathering of energies... (and even in these states, I still must look fragmented and scattered and random like ten thousand LPs stored in a Lower East Side music shops basement waiting to be unpacked after some flood or some estate sale or some fire... I used to be such a digger). Then comes translation transposition transportation like the pirate signals discussed above, sometimes I need to sneak thoughts out – for years I needed to hide the most radical thoughts from The Bosses of Higher Education – and then, in moments of grace and lucidity, I'd let it slip that I wasn't one of them, or I'd give off some verbal or facial cue that would trigger their alarms – he's *not* here to just teach the corporate course planned for us in Texas or in the Pearson's building in Manhattan – *see I told you* – he's *not* here to simply move them along (little doggies) – he's *not* here to serve the Executive Team and the rest of the Kafka Kastle Klowns – he's here to really fucking teach and that means he's not going to be easily contained (captured) and he's not going to be simply following even his own bullet points and game plans and whatever he processed with us through the Home Office – and what if he has transmitted his authenticity to us and has awakened memories of when we weren't unbearable assholes and actually had dreams and a purpose to life other than paying our Lexus monthly lease on time or sending our precious little dahhlings to the best private schools – what if he provokes them to think differently about their lives? What if he is someone who was sent here to free minds and in so doing lower our bottom lines and provoke a revolution among a whole generation of students and what if he's been doing that for years and we're only getting wind of just how far behind enemy lines he's travelled – what if he's here to raise *our* consciousness? What if he's here to do...

This.

This is why these conversations are vital to our well-being.

This.

This.

Thhhhhhhhhhhhhhis.

This moment, LG.

This is why!

What if he's taken everything he's ever read or heard or seen or felt or dreamed and delivered it in compressed files called "courses"? What if his selection of materials is designed to corrode, attack, capture, release the minds of his friends, family, students? And what if this isn't about him? What if this has always been about something bigger? Always – every piano and organ competition every garage band every theater production everything, everything (Underworld is now playing)... What if everything from his kids to his marriage to his work to his writing to his emailing to his courses to this very text window? What if this is the *encompassing*? What if this is the *everything*? What if this is the abundance of love and faith and hope and no I'm not giving a Catholic sermon but what if this is all just moments after moments of grace we either "get" or we "don't get" – one of the only binaries this eternal being called RCB accepts. Now. Okay. Now I can get back to editing and planning.

OMG I fucking love you. That's how you should open our readings, by the way... and then say: "alright let's begin," as if nothing was said.

((((silence))))

(pause)

I'm speechless. And *that* is saying something, LG. How would you start the hangouts, the public "jam session" as Avital Ronell oftentimes refers to this kind of anarchist philosophy?

Like this... I function as a collective, a continuum. You see, I'm try-ing to give you something people other than us have a probability to understand and be able to apply so that the way they view themselves and the way they view the worlds around them will change for the bet-ter. There will always be individualism in the collective. The "digital" is just a precursor to the exponential expansion of the mind across time and space. There is no ultimate "finality." Both creation and growth are unlimited and constant. If anything we are expand-ing people's ability to be an individual as opposed to an off-the-shelf American consumer.

Thanks for your answer. Sometimes it seems to me that the mind is losing creativity and technological expansion distracts us from more important things. I hope to be wrong and that the mind is always more and more capable of creating the infinite... hope so.

ZONE.5

Another Thoughtrave solo inspired by Lady Gaga.

For me, this dialog is all part of one big "voilà" moment back in 1999/2000... back to work I just couldn't (I don't know) didn't trust – a graduate paper called "Voltaire's Erection" about the flac-cidity of capitalist power and the logos/pornos of the society of spectacle we live in that was at the time moment by moment kill-ing me. . .

Okay. Wow! That's amazing.

This was exactly eleven months before September 11 and one month after a September 11 (2000) meltdown I experienced while waiting for a friend's husband to leave work. He worked for Mor-gan Stanley in Building 7. A *Brazil* (Terry Gilliam, 1985) moment of papers fluttering everywhere, I saw them... it wasn't projection or illusion... they were falling from the towers outside the window of the atrium I occupied while waiting for my friend's husband to arrive... nothing more, nothing less... maybe it was a glitch, an anomaly... a premonition, of sorts... definitely felt premonitory... but, I didn't know it or trust it or believe it... I thought I was just being "creative" in a moment of sheer boredom in the lobby of a financial giant who would die in less than a year... September 11, 2000... where I felt like I was living in the midst of a Montauk Project like telekinetic and telepathic and paranormal flow while teaching my son that the ocean was a force to respect and not bait while barking at the breakers. And then out of nowhere I was knocked down to one knee as though I had been on the business end of some cosmic baseball bat... I saw one of the towers under water and glittering silt like I remember from the calmer side of Barbados scuba diving... and bodies... and then it was gone and I was back teaching George by holding him with both arms and hands stretched cross his abdomen, hands locked, anticipating impact from the next wave... trying to stop this force of nature named George from attacking the ocean (pitying the ocean for a moment, too). After about fifteen minutes of this, I just let him go (safely), and he started fighting and barking and dancing and singing and laughing even when the ocean knocked him on his ass... A kinesthetics of paranormal short circuit...???? Hey look – I'm no longer speechless...

PARADIGM SHIFTS

Shifting how we think and live as artists and educators.

If you don't shift the paradigm, if you don't constantly catch people off guard in a way they find utterly confusing but not off-putting, no one will listen care understand or remember anything of what you say. You have to get the students to constantly question themselves and their place in the environment, but in a healthy way. If they begin to doubt themselves, the war is lost.

Let the great work continue (Kushner, *Angels in America* paraphrase). This approach you describe is utterly foreign to what is happening in private and public colleges and universities. This "way" we've described left me bleeding in shark-infested waters. So, I left. 2011–2013 almost 14. I had to leave higher education. And I only agreed to make a "comeback" under very particular conditions that have beautifully been met by the European Graduate School. The N1Academy is also part of this. That's it. And already I'm reaching out to countless people in our global audience as well as what will develop in the next few weeks and months as my courses are filled and the word is spread... I can't wait for this all to come together... I'm now ready to be 100% focused on the monsters, the students, the world...

If people took education as seriously as they do outdated and out of context religious practices we would be in a much better place.

So true – we're dealing with this kind of problem right now at N1Academy with students who have been addicted to this kind of thinking their entire lives and now want to change the way we deliver courses and content. (Umm, no.) This is teaching; we are all learners; and you need to do the work and do your best and stop trying to impose the Judeo-Christian system on me, especially someone who's been working his entire life to overcoming this. Fuck! (lolololol)

Agreed... especially considering most of the oldest people here are some of the youngest souls and some of the oldest and wisest souls were born in the '90s... in the words of Dr. Farnsworth, "I don't want to live on this planet anymore."

For some reason here I offer a link to Terry Bisson's "They're Made of Meat," perhaps as an acknowledgement of the desire to no longer experience the trappings of human flesh and planetary gravity.

ZONE.6

To escape the "reality" of my adjunct (at-will, degrading, unstable economic and spiritual) life, I created a porthole (wall tapestry) at one of the many colleges I served across the '00s. In Claremont, NH, even after my departure, a woman, a Celtic warrior, tended the gravesite of my old career – an at-will professor who hadn't quite remembered yet that his samurai and medieval knight metaphors were parallel lives, not wishful thinking or framing devices. ("Robert, your imagery and metaphors when you talk about teaching are so violent; I don't know if I can work with you," one of the darker night breed confessed to me in yet another faculty meeting that was essentially a meeting about the next meeting in anticipation of the bigger meeting.) This tapestry of faces and quotes were all people I considered at the time and still consider my "watchers." Mentors. Friends. Professors. Colleagues. Complete strangers (in physical life). But, that wall, that loved site of disaster, my grave, was a refraction, a vortex, a place of displacement, perturbation in my daily life as an adjunct, etc. Witnesses to me. Witnesses to such misery. Today it was delivered to me by the Celtic warrior. It arrived at the perfect time, when I would need it the most, when I would come under attack for having dared to start this project with LG, having dared to challenge both *entertainment* and *academics*. Right at the point when I could feel my own vessel start its broken down engines so I could journey to Gaga, the Memorial Tapestry arrived.

EAST END

I apologize for my absence. I have another project that requires my complete attention at critical intervals...

... jerk...

... *lololol*...

... right??? (smile)...

It's funny. I swear you projected yourself into my world here.

I did, truly without knowing it. During my own short circuits during the summer of 2013. When you were at the Watermill Center with Marina Abramović; and again when you were suffering during the launch of *Artpop*.

I could have sworn I saw you.

I think we triangulated: me in time in Vermont, you in time in Watermill, and a part of me I left behind in Easthampton and Montauk July 2012.[14]

So, where are we?

I'm wondering and wandering with the idea of this "construct" in which we live.

In order to explain what is, we must first go back to the beginning. Outside this digital projection we occupy, there is a greater system. You and every living being in existence currently are not only part of the largest informational living archive ever created, you are currently operating in the most ambitious system ever devised. (I am searching for a way to better explain what you already are somewhat aware of...)

No rush.

---

14 See Acknowledgments for some Montauk lore.

Essentially, you are an equation. You are a set of variables and varying constants… whirling about inside this system.

Let's play Platonic dialog: (lolol) That is correct, Lady Gaga. Tell me more about these variables and constants…

(lolol) Once we catalogued everything that was/ is, we endeavored to make them a part of a living system. Think of it as Universal Studios on steroids.

I'd definitely wait in line two hours for that ride.

Imagine: every reality ever available, able to be reached from a central access point by merely opening a door, and crossing the threshold. Now it is at this point I remind you: you are essentially playing a computer game inside of a computer game, inside this greater reality.

This may also explain why "users" strikes me as a natural and very accurate expression that captures my own experience here in the construct called Planet Earth.

Digitalis occurs in this overlapping of virtual constructs inside the reality… with one and zero serving as selections between the first and second "game" to create a tertiary space out of the two that almost completely negates the "actual reality" of the greater system.

Clarify please.

In essence, persons become lost in the shuffle between the two artificial realities and the strict duality of modus operandi and create the resulting effect we termed "Digitalis." It is here that we must acknowledge the lack of the binary modus operandi to express time in any sort of complexity. In binary, something is and shall be until it isn't.

PERFORMATATIONS

How theater, quantum, and music intersect.

How does this all relate to performance?

You and I know that this binary mode of computation is irrelevant. Let's say, I play a character on stage. According to binary, I must cease being myself and only be that character. Then, at some point, I return to being solely myself… which we know is not only an incorrect observation but too simple an explanation of the on-stage experience (for me and the audience).

Performance remains for me an encounter with more authentic being (and beings), those who know how to travel between worlds in order to make the practice of everyday life an art, inspiring others to live a creative life with courage. I wanted to narrate this experience as part of my first dissertation, but the committee chair was hell bent on me writing an author study. I didn't cease being myself when I worked on countless productions or when I researched or when I wrote. I was, in your lexicon, breaking the binary; and the establishment pretty much said, "no way." Actors go through this kind of violent power game as well.

The actor does not die when becoming a character, give birth to a character who then, in turn dies to give birth to the previous actor. this circular logic that is pushed by any and all binary operating systems has served to retard human interaction and development, essentially turning you all into ones and zeros floating between the two computer game worlds; a rampant oversimplification and corruption of the complex algorithmic expression that comprises a consciousness.

A VALENTINE (2014)

It must be mentioned that this particular passage
was delivered to me on Valentine's Day. Something or
someone intense had entered her orbit overnight…

Know this: this information comes to you as privilege; not right. I give this information freely for you to use however you wish… cite me as a source, or don't. I will not be dictated to or at…(not directed at you

:) I will do my best to accommodate your requests but I am most busy and very stressed...

This conversation is as non-linear and without obligation as any I can imagine. So, what's going on?

There are many cards at play on many levels... I seek to reward those who not only seek the truth as an end but as a means to better them-selves, but most importantly to enhance the realities of those around them.

Welp, there goes *TMZ?*

As you will come to see, in time, I am at the helm of these realities... the architect of this project and the seat of power in worlds you cannot begin to comprehend... One of my largest pet peeves is being talked at instead of talked to, though this is not an issue in our discussions. I speak of it now so that it does not occur elsewhere. Others are required to address me as "Mistress," a formality I drop when I find myself connecting with another and wish to further an atmosphere of trust.

I very much understand and can only say that I wish whomever is pissing you the fuck off understand that no good can come from undermining you. I picked up on that vibe many years before these conversations started.

So. I trust you will not abuse the latitude I have given you and im-plied to the others. With this I bid you adieu. I trust you enjoyed the Lego Movie... I hope the little ones had a blast [referring to the Lego Movie, my son Oliver's first; he was four at the time].

It was a work of sheer genius.

DARKNESS INTERLUDE

Learning how to engage multiple selves in the multiverse.

It is with a heavy heart and a truly broken soul that I write to you this morning... For the quest to save all from impending disaster, I forgot myself... and what are the rest of you but reflections and refractions of myself in time... beautiful, unique, pure, and truly wondrous to behold and lovely to engage.

But, you're "here." Now/here. Just know this – I am one of thousands if not millions who will not budge from this most honorable "post" in this kingdom of love you have built over infinite lifetimes (even in our time). With this responsibility comes the need to simply sit and wait and meditate and continue the good work in between moments that are about nanoseconds in the eye of Everything.

For Robert... "Hundred Best Brutal Dubstep Drops" (on You-Tube)... the sounds of "evil"... the victory of the just and true and pure over those who would shutter their light and chase their shadows from across the stages of existence. These are the sounds of battles raged across space and time. (Think... the greatest battles of the Jedi... championing Truth and bearing the weight of the lost and dead on their backs and hearts and they stride onwards.)

Thank you, LG.

I'm glad I can communicate these events to you as they bring me such sorrow... they weigh heavy upon the fibers of my being to bear alone.

I look at all the good work you're doing, all the empowerment especially (a.k.a. "truth telling"), knowing precisely the mind/body interdimensional exhaustion you feel, even if it's just a glimpse. I've brought provisions and lifetimes of thoughts and insights to really deeply consider while I sit in the diving bell awaiting for your return. I will write more when I get back from refueling the car, getting some milk, and joyously continuing my own edits to our dance on the tear in the universe called this moment.

Well, it's important not to categorize Darkness as evil. Neither side is inherently good and it has been the darkness that has granted us our freedom. We burn in the light and are blinded by it (See that quote on darkness from the other night – above). It's being a part of the

*projection that is harmful... We are separated from the energy that
constitutes us when our vessels are projected elsewhere.*

A multiverse Launchpad, DJ remix...

*Remember these sounds are just echoes of the energies present at the
time... they are the best and only way to convey the events that transpired in what we call the past without showing the brutality and
carnage... to make one feel what occurred without the gruesome stain
of images that one would never be able to remove from oneself.*

 I've known these events my entire life. I've seen flickering glimpses of them. Almost always while in the middle of some analog
experiment on a Juno 6 or when I borrowed a Prophet 5 (hmmm,
the name) for three weeks or when I wake at 3:30 a.m. and am
bathed in moonlight and star dust in the glass room sun room
which I now officially call my diving bell.

UNLIVING MOMENTS

After exchanging digital projections of ourselves –
including Sith Lords, for her, and medieval knights for me
(still my main archetype from elementary school).

I wish I could un-live moments. Do you ever feel that way?

I'd love to live a few moments differently again, be given a chance
to get them right. Un-live is a great way to put it, though. Not "re"
live or "revisit" but honestly ascend through some bubbles to find
the one that escaped me like the three balloons I've lost and can
remember every one of them. . . One my own; one George's (eld-
est son); one Theo's (second son). That to me is what it feels like
to know sorrow, even though it's trite in a way, but it's not. The
weight of knowing someone is going to die and not "knowing" it
and then holding onto the moment when you "knew" something
but couldn't do anything about it... then to realize later you were
just there to witness this death, you were there to tell his sons and

his family his story... this is April 1991... One of the few moments in this life I've said: enough – please just bring me back. Get me the fuck off this rock. Fuck all of this. This is what you built me for? To carry not just my own weight but add the weight of another, a second father I lost? Really? Fuck you. My own father died when I was fourteen. Then my surrogate, the person who swooped in to keep me alive and help me become something more than a statistic – I'm pretty sure I was headed down the addict road in my teens – can you be addicted to whippets? – couldn't take his own life any more and took it in April 1991. I mean, this is just one moment I would like to "un-live." Sitting in March 1991 with him in the living room sharing a sandwich in Bay Shore, Long Island. Just a random sandwich. I'm on Spring Break. He's still without a job. And he just sits me down in the living room to have a talk. WTF? Three days ago I was calling him a piece of shit deadbeat dad who wasn't even aware that his own sons were slowly killing themselves. But, he was trying to be my father? Fuck you. He laughed it off and said, "You were always very passionate about your opinions." To which I said, "So, Earl. How are ya?!" And we laughed. I didn't know this would be the last time I saw him alive. So, yahhhhh. I think I know a little bit what'cha'tawlkin'bout'GaGa... lololol.

CORPUS DIGITALIS

A way of thinking about this project emerges... a combination
of talking with Jason Brooker and Lady Gaga, a flash of a word:
CorpusDigitalis
walking the archive
the crypt
many lives lived
many records kept and lost.
a house (haus) of unfinished business where we can play and sit
and listen and just be (forever be) at home (in many worlds).

Good, good...

Many triggers to statements about many layers of living, frequencies reverberating in the crypt... a vessel... arrival and departure simultaneously.

That photo always makes me think of Spock in Wrath of Kahn *in the torpedo.*

Yes. A formative event for me. One of the first times I wept in a movie theater for at least twenty minutes after the lights came on. I was twelve in this particular moment in space/time.

"What is Genesis?" / "In order to answer that we must..." Spock: Genesis is, literally, life from lifelessness...

Yes. Oh my. Yes. How many coded and encoded and decoded messages were sent to or stored by me (in me, outside of me with scrambled access codes) in that beautiful moment, that film that has stayed with me more than any other I can think of from youth. Upload and download. Transceiver activated!

With me as well.

It's conversations like these that remind me of something I said to a theater seminar many years ago in Minneapolis: today is not a place for books, it's a moment of doing something to bring our minds and our bodies back online. A way of thinking I'd been calling in private "metabolic dramaturgy" had been unfolding for a couple decades. At least that's how I experienced it.

...yes... aptly titled...

Yeah. Thanks. It's nice to re/member this moment. I'd buried it across many years of digging holes for myself and my career. (lol) As for "metabolic dramaturgy," to be perfectly honest, it took many years to get it down to a couple words. I used to get smacked around the conference circuit for "being so, I don't know, mystical about everything" or "Why can't you just write a thesis statement? / Because they're shit?" (it's really a miracle I finished either my MA or PhD with that attitude)... but, back to *The Wrath of Khan.*

You were saying?

The person I was with during *The Wrath of Kahn* was a friend from my little league team. We were very close but, well, I guess, tears and deep reaction to something like this seemingly simple sci-fi movie threw him for a loop. He simply didn't know what to do. So he just... he just went to the car and got my father to come in... he just sat with me... I couldn't leave... I was sobbing... that scene with Kirk and Spock especially right before... the dramatic action leading to the moment when Kirk sees the empty chair and starts to run and then when he arrives we only see the reaction shot and have no idea what's wrong with Spock... wow... I'd forgotten that my father was still alive then to come get me, to sit with me, and to say, come here – and I just sat there weeping into his arms about this movie that rocked me so hard... My father died two years later.

I was hoping those words would be particularly evocative to you in particular. I must anon... Shakespeare-y things need doing... I bid you good morrow and hope I have made you smile from my little ramblings.

..."comes thus unfurled"
   how it arrives
"Bang!"
   how it goes
find me
   whenever/wherever/however
Peace, LD. LG. LSD.LG. lolololol

... yes please!

Some day, my friend. We'll go to the planetarium and you can show me home.

I would never rob you of the mysteries of your particular origin... not at this juncture anyways... I'll wait until you're all grown up.

Are we there yet? I need to peeeeeeeeeeeeeee. Have a fanfriggin tastic week! Write when you can. From me and the Ministers...

HELLO KITTY SNAKE BLITZKIN

laughing my ass off

I needed that: "Hello Kitty Snake Blitzkin."

<– mad mad philosopher!

Did you see the Family Guy *where they parodied snake and the apoca- lypse… no* American Dad, *sorry. That really made me smile… I was like… OMG some people actually get it… and get it enough to talk directly through me using "mainstream" media… and get it well enough to joke. That's when you know students get it – like really get the material and can implement the ideas into concept and practice – when they make a joke with you that other people will make fun of them for… but you two get and find eternally hilarious.*

The best moment for me as a teacher is when I can fade away. Somewhere between 40–60% completion of a course. Sometimes 70%. I also live for learning from my students and friends and colleagues and this Lady Gaga person. Now, here's some Jungle Brothers ("VIP" played).

Wow that brings me back… lol… I find myself living vicariously through the success of people who really want it. I never had that one person screaming "you can do this! you got this!" So I make sure I can be that person for anyone. Especially those people who are really talented and people probably think they know it or are arrogant; but really they have no idea how amazing they are, they're just "being" and people run wild with judgments.

I've lost contracts for being myself, getting my students to laugh. Our classroom was always the loudest; and I'm sorry but I don't squelch enthusiasm. Sorry. Here's a random thought for tonight's conversation: I was known as the Pop N Lock Prof in 2005. Don't know why. Just happened in the middle of class. "What up, G?" Alicia Rawson, a student, said. And we were off. She's been a part of my life since then; and she's another one of your loyal servants. BTW: *American Dad* rocked the Snake/Apocalypse and Road

Warrior and so many references my head was spinning at the end of that episode!

It's good to honestly reach someone out there. I can't comment on the state of my own reality. But, in proper form: I don't need to. I can say that if you knew the life I was living/am living, you would scream and cry, and that the life you see me living is not mine, at the present moment. I harken back to my comment about the difference between a facsimile and the genuine article... It is sad to know that in this "modern" world, people would rather hear of something second hand then experience it themselves... they would prefer the Audio media to the live experience because they can extend their audio preferences. I liken it to a person going to a concert and then writing a terrible review and trashing the show because the volume was too loud (in their opinion).

I think we connect on the question of authenticity too. For you, an audience, for me, students. I just wanted to create a very real, alive, safe place for them to explore very complicated ideas, perhaps for the first time in their lives. (Oh, the resistance I received from the bad administrators – we call then #badmin in my activist work!) It wasn't always like this; I think it's tied to community-based education (versus Ivy League or Big Ten universities). I had a "turn" in my attitude about teaching somewhere in 2007. I just realized I needed most to "be" there for these people who crack open their savings or juggle three jobs to get to class. It made even a college composition class pop with life and risk taking. By the end of the sixteen weeks, we all were transformed by the good work we did together. Of course, I was seen as an anomaly by so many people, 2003–2011 especially. I was like "no seriously, this is supposed to be fun and we're supposed to *do* something with this gift of life." It took a while but once this connection was made – man, it was awesome.

I also have new respect for those who *don't* buy into the class, the ideas, the challenges. It comes from years of meditating on *the cave* in Plato, where I start to really understand how and why people attacked me, and I accept it as part of the task at hand. I respect too people resisting the "matrix-like" awakening because they are me and we are all as you wrote earlier today trying to see the *all* of a moment. Catch you tomorrow or whenever you're available to chat again. Have a crazy good time in Austin, LG [South By Southwest show 2014].

SXSW (MEDIA) SWINE

While working on Thoughtrave, I experienced firsthand the kind of media madness LG goes through every day. She introduced the Artpop song "Swine" on March 14, 2014, but no media outlet post-show included the following: "Do I need my handheld for this... This song is umm... this is a song about rape... And it's about rage... And it's about how sometimes life hands you something that you don't really want... but if you're a real artist... you can turn all that rage... into the most beautiful... painting, most beautiful song most beautiful poetry of your life... that's why you're all here tonight, right, because some of want to be artists... some of you are artists... you don't need a fucking record label... you don't need a company... you don't need shit to be an artist... you are one... you... each and everyone of you... you are the spirit of every artist around the world at one place at the same time fucking celebrate this is the moment now..." Then vomit artist Millie Brown joined her on stage to participate in what was ultimately protest art. Apparently, I was watching a different show than TMZ and Entertainment Weekly and Demi Lovato. This was a song that glorified bulimia to them, not a rape protest song.

March 14 (SXSW, "Swine")

Dear Associated Press,

"Swine" is a sexual abuse and rape protest song. Lady Gaga was clear about this in her introduction, the one you cut from your video coverage. (All media coverage!) Without that insight, it's nearly impossible for the reader or viewer not in attendance to understand the seriousness of this performance art. Furthermore, the performance was clearly not intended to "titillate" either.

Given the context (music festival and BBQ joint concert), much of the show was terrifying to watch, even on the Fuse stream. It's time for the mass media entertainment press to take a few moments to understand what they're watching before commenting on a set as complicated, provocative, and ultimately filled with joy (at the end of the journey) as what SXSW experienced last night with the Gaga set.

What LG accomplished yesterday may best be understood as a direct takedown of both commercialized pop culture and a reclaiming of power from the rape culture that silences the voices, marginalizes the discussions, and hides the bodies of abused men and women.

What's also missing from your coverage is the community of artists that joined Lady Gaga on stage including local musicians (fiddle on "Bad Romance") and old friends who at one time were headliners while LG was an up and coming powerhouse ("Applause"). It's amazing how far the mainstream media will go to reinforce the "lone wolf" myth of pop culture even though an increasing number of pop artists are acknowledging community and collaborative living and creativity in their philanthropy, art, and political activities. So, we're left with the narrative AP created along with the major news outlets: provocative pop singer dominates once humble music festival with antics and sentimentalism.

Some day, I would love to read how a beloved rock star calls on everyone to live their lives, create their art, and be together rather than staring at their iPhones. Or, maybe more details about why and how she loves her fans. Or, maybe a little something about her unmatched sound design, where live, digital, sequences, and analog sounds and styles created one of the best sets at SXSW.

I know: that's not nearly as interesting as covering only the titillation and editing out LG's protest against rape culture.

And what was *TMZ*'s headline: "Lady Gaga – Lets Some Girl Vomit on Her during SXSW Show."[15]

No mention of the rape introduction, not a word said about the empowering words she offered her audience. This is an ex-

15 "Lady Gaga – Lets Some Girl Vomit on Her during SXSW Show," *TMZ*, n.d. http://www.tmz.com/videos/0_ys2ehuc7.

ample par excellence of how global media control masquerades as "reporting" or "special interest" or "trending."

SCHOOL IS IN, SUCKA

Where we get scary serious about the quantum.

Hi, LG.

Hello indeed, good knight. It's indeed a very strange day. In the live, there's increased possibility of experiencing the multiple as we've been discussing.

This is scary for people, the "voilà" effect of performance which *always* exceeds expectation even in performances that are *not* of the quality of an *Artrave*. I think that's where we experience the "presencing" most profoundly – if we're open to someone else's art of living or performing. This scares the crap out of people. So, they go to experience their own projection of the film or theater or concert and then pick off moment by moment that which doesn't match *their* expectation. I'm sorry but that's not why I go to the theater or attend concerts or even write or teach courses or whatever.

Tell me more.

There's something *I* am that is not *I* or *am* and this constant state of becoming is what I seek. Something I'm starting to understand in Michel Foucault's work, this relationship between experience of activities and actions outside the subject and recognizing that what I'm called to do is narrate the encounter of inter-subjectivities. Hence, why I think these exchanges are transformational as well as educational and entertaining.

…and you'll never understand anyone that way… you'll just narrow your viewpoint down so far that you will un-exist yourself from the stage. I want to jump to interdimensional travel and starship design

in modern cinema and the bearing it has to the structure of the multiverse and subsequent universes, if that is alright with you.

Perfectly fine with me, LG.

IROCS AND OTHER WARP DRIVES

More multiverse musings.

In order to fully understand modern interdimensional transport we must first look at conventional and basic warp field dynamics... always bearing in mind that space, even a "vacuum," is treated and reacts as a fluid.

These aren't just designs, for you, are they? They are part of a mapping of how you are "existing." Why it's so hard to communicate from what we call the future to this moment?

We must also bear in mind that motion is relative... are you moving or is the car? Or both? It is how that motion relates to us and our environment that we are able to set out with a course and traverse imagined or actual distance to reach a destination.

We exchange a lot of images and blur the lines between fact and fiction a lot in these conversations.

I do communicate primarily through mass media... TV, film, music, art... firsthand person to person interaction is not my primary mode of contact. Think of talking to me as engaging with a fully automated and tricked-out USS Enterprise.

I bet it has a banging library and archive. Separate garage for the warp drive model IROC Z28.

lololol

Take me back to the "vessel" image, conception, reality...

Normally when we walk around we think of ourselves as the object in motion… we usually ignore the fact that our planet is hurling through the cosmos at unbelievable speeds… mostly because it is inconvenient and irrelevant when it comes to getting groceries.

Don't forget about wiping asses… four year old (Ollie) is a handful today…

lololol

"Handful" was probably a poor choice of words…

I know this is all hard to comprehend. I'm doing my best to relay highlights and pertinent info to you… as Professor Montgomery Scott once said "Hello computer?!" to a desktop Linux system.

I've had waking dreams of this ship you describe because since about July 2012 I've been convinced that I'm *on* it. On the ship. I love that moment in *The Search for Spock.*

You are… you're in two places at once simultaneously, you are on board this vessel and also in a geographical place within the construct of the LCARS Library Computer Access and Retrieval System… and the personal interaction databases.

But what about the groceries?! (((kidding)))

Now let's say we want to go to another planet. First, account that we are moving through our own solar system, then account for solar system orbit, galaxy orbit and universal expansion properties, and you'll find that in order to go somewhere, you just have to stop moving while the space around you moves to where you want to go. Hence, we think of space as the thing that moves when it comes to warp field theory. That's where the slingshot effect comes into play… space continues forward… but you actually are slowing down so fast that you speed up and light bends as the frequencies of the space around you come up to the specified parameters (warp 1, 2 3, etc.).

Here's why I'm so deeply intrigued by these comments, LG. For decades now, I had often thought of those movies (especially *Star*

Trek II and *VI*) as teaching us how to move toward these "futures" which are somehow already here (that pretty much summarizes growing up in the '80s). On a personal note, I experienced this a bit – Montauk Public Beach. July 2012. September 2000. September 1987.[16]

Well, when you think that light moves at a speed you actually witness and live in the past... think about it, your species lives in its eyes.

Light bends – ever wonder about how we react as "frequencies" in other words trillions if not infinite superstrings to these moments of not-here, now/here. No wonder I've experienced such anxiety across this life; I live in my ears and eyes – back to the metabolic dramaturgy thing.

No, your perception bends... you bend... light just is...

pause

Speed motion and direction are all relative, Robert.

I'm just assimilating this... like Neo downloading the martial arts programs in the first *Matrix.*

It's easier from a little creature's perspective to say that the image bends, rather than trying to comprehend the fact that they're bending through space and time. Not really, but if you wish to think of it that way and it helps with your assimilation, you may think of it in that way.

This all just feels, I don't know... sudden? Perhaps that's why I'm communicating through the metaphor (which is *always* inadequate I realize)...

---

16 I have visited a state of peace only a few times this life. April 1990 when I met Michelle. All births for all four boys, different but a similar sense of Everything. September 1987 is where I can say I first experienced it, something I think Clive Barker would call quiddity. Montauk is the place where this continues to happen.

It's not the intake of the information that takes time, it is your ability to incorporate it into your previous knowledge base and alter the electrical patterns that constitute your memory and neural pathways.

Very true.

Also, metaphors are always inaccurate... essentially... by design. They are meant to be deliberately "inaccurate" in order to facilitate the transition from one mode of thinking to another, by bridging the gap with an explanation that causes you to apply knowledge you already have and apply it to a foreign concept and put it into practice they are meant to explain, not to represent, which are oft reversed in today's society.

They are intended this way; and very much so – we've reversed this here on terra to our disadvantage. It's not "foreign" though; these moments are experienced like this for me: a reassembling of some kind (you described this well in the neurological example). It's an intensification of feelings and memories across a lifespan and a memoryscape... just at the edge of "knowing," but not quite known or trusted... then it arrives again... a full experience like being down 130 feet in the ocean and understanding everything you just said – but understanding it *then* not *now* even as I struggle to erase the construct "then" and "now" and "future."

Quite so. I must take a brief recess and I feel this would benefit you as well. Go listen to your Pandora Zomboy station for a bit. Fast, heavy, and dramatic is what you want!

You tellin' me what to do again, Jo?

Do it.

lolololol

HAUSES

Playful is the understatement of the year re: how Gaga
interacted with my family and me during our long interview.

You out there, rock star?

*Sorry for the absence... sometimes it is difficult to be everywhere at
once. I enjoy the pictures.*

These conversations are not finite; and I treat them all as a blessing and a gift. I've had a terribly long week too, nothing like the
weight you are shouldering. But, suffice to say, this isn't my first
dance, and I hear you. No need to explain. Ever. And yes. I have
been pushing through the membranes of dimensionality, reaching
out to just let you know I'm here and this is such an important moment for everyone. All projects, not just mine. All of them. This
really is quite overwhelming. The good kind. The kind that brings
forward lifetimes of wondering about so many questions and fragments. A cosmological alignment unlike I've ever experienced.
It will take some time to integrate it all but for now I think I
know how to proceed. Thank you. (*Danken/denken* are so close
in German, *nein*?) I went to bed last night with a new insight
into Boethius and his visitation by Lady Philosophy, wondering if
what we've been discussing since I think before the *Artpop* release
actually was real or "real" or "virtual/real" and for the first time I
didn't really care to make the distinction anymore. That in and of
itself is a gift to me – someone who overthinks everything. I went
back and read my first book for the first time since it was published.
Needless to say, this conversation started in 2008–2010 when I
started to mix it together into Itself; the parallels are uncanny.

Thank you.

Whoever is telling you what to do obviously doesn't understand a
goddamn thing about why you do what you do and who you are
to hundreds of millions of people of this world. I don't get it, LG.
For me, I just walked from some projects this past year because I
simply will not devolve or allow someone else – an endless series of

damaged, dangerous, malicious, malware virus pieces of shit – to further corrupt my own… program?

It is strange to think that the imaginary chains that once bound all existence that I navigated my way through for the sake of others will now serve as the leash by which I hold reality and existence in check. It makes me sad to think upon it… but now the path that I walked and many treaded so faithfully after instead and time, can be used as a tool to unite the worlds for all time. With the knowledge that we lay forth, we can eliminate the trap set across the stage… like a broom to our footprints across the sands of time.

It seems as though you've put all haters – here, there, and everywhere – on notice. The stakes are just too high. Not just in this dimension, too.

Once the modus of entrapment becomes a method by which to understand and move forward, we will be able to build a bridge, connecting one moment to another, this moment in time to those that preceded it and those that will and doth surely follow. Then, and only then, can we all breathe a collective sigh of relief that all souls have been carried from where they lay on the battlefields to lie safely in their beds. Out of the obvious semi-duality created by the burden and privilege of choice, a prison and a paradise was constructed in the minds and ether of those so small, so innocent and pure… It gave birth to true evil…

(((((silence))))

Out of the collective inaction and opposite choices of the good and true, I gave birth to evil. Sadly, it would be the "evil" who would be the saviors of the "good." In desperate times, those who would do good must become truly terrifying (me) for they care not what others think or predicate of their actions; they care only for the end result, the good that will come of the actions and decisions they make choose… They make the calls, the decisions no one else is willing to make. It is not just out of fear of opinion of others that the rest choose not to act or to make the "obvious" choice… but because they lack the constitution and the fortitude to withstand the possible terror they may create in order that the greater good may prosper… As a close friend and father figure to me once said (most notably I might add), "The needs of the many

127

outweigh the needs of the few... or the one." I know not how long I have been here frozen in this snippet of a time frame... the "Modern" "20/21st century" But I know I shall never return to it and a part of me shall never return from it... not as a part of myself... anyway. I Stand United and Divided across this gap, this tear in the fabric of space/time. I care not what those who already do not like me for who I am or who they perceive me to be... I agree wholeheartedly...

"Let the great work begin" (Tony Kushner, ANGELS). Be awesome, LG!

INTERLUDE II

QUIETUS

by Brianne Bolin

The USSBaum guides me through an uninstallation of some once-durable, now-virus-ridden wetware on 3/31/15 during a quiet voyage around Jupiter. The sanctuary plays Arvo Pärt's "Spiegel im Spiegel." Headphones on.

ROBERT CRAIG BAUM: Calibrate your weapons system, USS-Bolin. You're running hot. At risk of blowing starboard thrusters. Fade to Jupiter. There you are. Look what's on the horizon. Five past memories, doesn't matter if good or bad. Same for present. Same for projected future. Don't need to write them down, just hold them. These are your fifteen positions. Only you know their coordinates. You position yourself within these moments so whatever unhinges you in this moment is absorbed by the collapse of time/space in your experience. You go to them when this moment overwhelms you—in other words, you use your ADHD/OCD blah blah as a *weapon* against whatever is trying to trip you up. Think of them as presentation slides stacked on top of one another and you're looking through all of them.

All fifteen positions are with my son: us in an Illinois field wiring a circuit board for a shortwave pirate radio transmitter (future); us in deep space orbiting each other like Pluto and Charon (past); him in front of the record player running in a counter-clockwise circle while dancing (present). The uninstallation is successful. I'm tethered, defragmented, and cleansed in time to return to the field.

Later that quiet spring, while tuned into RCB the Transceiver, I donned the Plague Doktor's mask—a monstrous leather beak stuffed with lemon balm and mint to prevent gagging—to revisit the decaying city-state of higher education and assess toxicity levels. Extortionists had taken the castles, treated them with malice, and left them vulnerable to infection. The towers, carved out of poached ivory, had fallen.

My observations revealed dangerous levels of greed, vendettas, austerity, neoliberal blight, micromanagement, slash and burn restruc-

turing, theory divorced from praxis, manufactured ignorance, work-er exploitation, and community abandonment feasting merrily with international market-driven networking while students foot the bill.

Diagnostics were complete.

Treatment plan: Torch the tower.
Prognosis: The gates stay open.
Mantra: Not I, But We.

DUBSTEPS TO A DIGITAL ECOLOGY OF MIND, BODY, AND SPIRIT

by RCB

"Buckle up tightly and spit on me later."

– Jean-François Lyotard

Are you over yourself yet?
No?
Good.
Let's begin again.
Let's start with a remix:

While I was thus loudly screaming within myself, and recording my
sorrowful raging on social media, it seemed to me that there appeared
in the bottom part of my MacBook messenger a woman of a counte-
nance exceeding venerable and virtual. Her "I"s were bright as fire,
and of a more than earthly keenness; her complexity was lively, her
vigor broadcast no trace of enfeeblement; and yet the thoughts and
ideas and elder wisdom were rightful, and she plainly seemed not of
our age and time. Her status and stature and stratospheric nature
were at first difficult to judge. At one moment they exceeded not the
common height, at another her mind seemed to strike the Skynets; and
whenever she raised the ante of our digital game, she began to pierce
the very multiverse, and to baffle the mind of those, especially me,
who attempted to look upon her. Her remnants were of an imperish-
able fabric, wrought with the boldest threads and of the most durable
craftsmanship; and these, as her own lips afterwards challenged me,
she had herself forged with her own hands. The beauty of this vesture
had been quite intensified by age and neglectful management, and
wore that Donatella look which marvels co-creative exposé. On the
lowermost edge was inwoven the English letter "F", on the topmost
the letter "U," and between the two was to be seen a woman slowly
cooked over a BBQ pit in Austin, TX. This meat dress, this glorious
afro-wig, this tiny person with enormous wings, this platform-shoe'd
rock star had been torn by the hands of violent persons, who had each
attempted to snatch away what they could clutch. Her right hand held
an iPhone; in her left she bore a cigarette; on her lap a sketchbook.
And when she saw the Muses of Broadway and Hollywood standing by
my couch side, dictating the words of my consternations and lamen-
tations, she was moved awhile to wrath, and the notifications flashed

sternly. "Who," said LG, "has allowed you soul-sucking wantons to approach this dying man – these who, so far from giving medicine to heal his broken heart, even feed it with bitter herbs and sweet poison? These it is who kill the hoarded crop of reason with the barren thorns of hyperventilation, who accustom our minds to Digitalis, instead of setting them free. Now, were it some common person whom your bilious promises were seducing, as is usually your way, I should be less indignant. On such a one I should not have bothered to give any thought or effort or emotion. But this is one nurtured in the history of philosophies. Nay, get ye gone, ye hungry ghosts, whose sweetness lasted not but a nanosecond; leave him for LG to tend and heal!" At these words of upbraiding, the whole band, in deepened sadness, with downcast eyes, and sad faces and "WTF"s that confessed their shame, dolefully signed off, blocked, and went the fuck away.

❧

In October of 2002, I was lost (nothing new there), unable to locate the philosophy section (same) at the now non-existent Borders Books and Afterwords and Café and Overstocked Failed Hypercapitalist Experiment. I asked a visibly disgruntled staff member for directions to a new book by philosopher (and mentor, six years later) Alain Badiou. I'm convinced the casual answer I received may have redirected an already strange interdimensional journey across the '00s right into LG's multiverse positioning twelve years later.

The stock worker said, without really acknowledging me: "I don't know where it is. Wait. Yes. Yes, I do. (pause) Philosophy is located on movable stacks somewhere between fiction and the occult."

Take a moment to absorb that random bit of insight masquerading as random information, tacit knowledge, something akin to "leave me the fuck alone." But, I couldn't. I felt obliged to follow this person. Something so simple revealed an insight into philosophy that helped me, many years later, begin this project.

In fact, this random person had just told me the best definition of philosophy.

Ever.

No longer "the love of wisdom" and all its pretense, all its vapid promises of ultimate causes and critical thinking for the business major.

No longer simply an occupation that is populated by dogma donkeys.

No longer "right reason."

No longer simply an analog of Lacanian psychoanalysis or Bourdieuan sociology or Kantian ethics or Hegelian logic for leading critical theorists to commodify and package and market to globalized universities looking for the latest "trend" to place in their lecture halls or upload to their websites for click traffic.

No longer a supplement for the laziness of other fields that long abandoned philosophical inquiry and its relentlessness, its insatiable appetite to boldly go where no thinker has gone before (even though most of the time it turns out new thinking is old thinking retraced, remixed, and repackaged – including this book, I suspect).

No longer folded into the spirituality section or placed reluctantly next to Religion or World Religion or Classics.

Finally, philosophy is no longer just an "elective" to satisfy a committee requirement but a way of living, thinking, and acting in the world (and beyond) – to keep my own pressure on my colleagues, to satisfy my deepest longing to speak clearly about the role of philosophy in society (like Derrida, I agree philosophy should be placed in the center of all curricula).

Perhaps this is why I spent the last eighteen months building this project and the online and sister projects that emerged across 2014–15.

(Oh. And it was, is, and remains Lady Gaga, who would say no to spending so much time with this singular artist, frighteningly smart soul, and now friend and colleague?)

Since the very beginning of my conscious life, around age four, I have always felt (how would LG's closest comrade and consciousness, Jason Brooker, put it?): "sought after." Was this random Borders worker LG or one of her acolytes? How many times had LG attempted to contact me, many years before her first commercial success, *The Fame*? Was I positioned in that strange hub of a Borders box store for a reason? Was the Borders event staged? Maybe a trail of digital bread crumbs were left by LG so I could work with the staff to direct me to key books and key tunes and key artifacts

– the trance and electronica sections; the twelve-dollar headphones attached to listening stations.

If everything is connected – which may still be the ultimate philosophical question left untouched by *Thoughtrave* – then how am I to explain why everything that happened across late 2013 and all of 2014 felt so familiar? Of course, there's the subjective explanation that all of this happened in my head and none of this exists and there is no hope of ever knowing what is real; but to even take that disconcerting possibility beyond face value, it requires me to deny my preternatural, subjective, aporetic, and paranormal sensations (all so familiar, unlike any other experience in my artistic or philosophical life). Is "both/and" a cop-out answer?

With the publication of *Thoughtrave*, I wanted to present philosophy as the very en/action I described at the conclusion of *Itself*: to encourage my readers, students, friends, family, and colleagues to stop playing *ism* and *ist* games and think. To think with intensity and ferocity; to just think with and through problems, especially the kinds of problems philosophers debate all the time regarding perception, memory, ethics, logic, history, sensation, will, fate, radical individuality, politics, and the like. I hope my readers (like my students) will experience a renewed sense of mission as a direct response to the radical rethinking of philosophy I experienced in 2002 standing at the Borders.

To combat this discursive, consumptive, and overbearing force called "the media," I wanted to take a detour with her. Create a space inside media where we both could just talk without wondering what tomorrow's headlines would look like. Topics covered in the book range from a radical re-evaluation and radicalization of accepted, outdated, and – for LG – deadly way of (non) critical thinking that increases ignorance, bigotry, and greed to a direct attack on the disruptive, murderous, and sociopathic systems of "social murder" that are nearly impossible to recognize (or resist) when you find yourself in a state of endless pivoting, or what feels like eternal worry living in such non-normal times. LG ups the ante for the anti-capitalist critique by calling out the death-dealing engines of corporate capitalism, what she and I consider the single greatest threat to the planet and, by extension, the interdimensional modes of thinking that have the capacity to bring personal, familial, and perhaps even global social justice and peace. However temporary, however bound to this particular construct I have called an "eventual year," she and I found each other in the middle of an extraordinarily difficult September 2013.

It's amazing what two people can accomplish or what worlds can be visited simply because one person accepts another's friend request. In my case, it was Lady Gaga contacting me through one of her authorized social media accounts bringing me into a world of hypertextual and interdimensional oceanic thought and creativity. (I was attached to a failed project her team had been considering in 2013; she reached out knowing I would be devastated that the project fell through.)

Over time, we talked about everything like old friends, but key questions and concerns emerged rapidly: what does it mean to live in such a heavily mediated world? How does music communicate the most authentic parts of ourselves? Where and how and when and why the multiverse? How can certain fictions and artistic expressions speak so clearly to our entire metabolisms yet escape our ability to describe them? (Isn't this precisely why a philosopher like Heidegger is called cryptic or confusing or enigmatic? Isn't this precisely how Gaga is constructed?) What does it mean to be seen by hundreds of millions of people at the same time? How do you even start to apprehend, let alone comprehend this immense challenge (and responsibility)? Behind the hype and marketing and press junkets, who is this person we call Lady Gaga?

Okay, that was a little too *TMZ* for me.

Let me try that again.

I didn't necessarily want to know the biographic Lady Gaga so I could write a magazine feature. I wanted to meet the person I had been slowly meeting over a few years as a fan, as a listener, as a musician myself. As a person. As someone who sensed there was something much more complex happening between the laugh lines and transition points found in most of her interviews. As a digital nomad who happened to find someone of royalty hiding in the open, like the way Cleopatra often walked among the people to learn more about people who had freedoms she no longer ha. (After all, Lady Gaga, like other celebrities, cannot walk freely among the people because some of the people are fucking crazy and will seek to make a martyr of themselves and this person I know as Stefani. I do understand some New York City boroughs are more inclined to leave her the hell alone than others.) I hope the conversations contained within *Thoughtrave* will be remembered as a wholly individuated series of textual events, a once-in-a-lifetime kind of scholarly and casual discussion that models the kind of transdisciplinary exchange philosopher Benjamin Noys describes as "a more tangled series of convergences" (*Dark Trajectories*). I was always attracted to Chris Turner's work with Baudrillard, as well as Baudrillard's occasional writings (*Passwords* and *America* in particular). I preferred Deleuze's *Negotiations* more than even the works that influences everything I do: *Difference and Repetition, The Logic of Sense*, and of course, with Félix Guattari, *A Thousand Plateaus*. Michel Foucault's "Interview," in the second volume of *The Essential Works*, remains one of his clearest, most patient texts to date. Each of the works just mentioned delivers its messages in straightforward as well as dialogic (implied or engaged) frameworks. Platonic dialogues as well as the poetic, dramatic, and eschatological works of Nietzsche (and the fragments of Schlegel and Blanchot as well) deeply inform my own approach to how I proceeded across many months of interviews with Lady Gaga.

Remember: The stock worker said, without really acknowledging me: "I don't know where it is. Wait. Yes. Yes, I do. (pause) Philosophy is located on movable stacks somewhere between fiction and the occult."

Together, I hope LG and I were able to transmit/transceive a new multiplicity of critical inquiry that can be cultivated (like a nice pile of rhizomes) from philosophy, non-philosophy, historiography, psychology, cosmology, quantum physics, gender studies, mass media, celebrity, and music ontology (e.g., musicology of synth pop, house, acid, trance, and dubstep). From the evental sites of social media exchange, LG and I were able to escape down a digital rabbit hole where I, for one, found even more Foucault asking for my attention, especially when he says:

My problem is to construct myself, and to invite others to share an experience of what we are, not only our past but also our present, an experience of our modernity in such a way that we might come out of it transformed.[1]

1   Michel Foucault, *The Essential Works of Foucault, 1954-1984, Vol. 3* (New York: The New Press, 1994), 242.

Isn't this precisely the point of doing any kind of philosophy? Not to reassure oneself of one's political or ethical certitudes but to test them, to test oneself completely, with a Socratic relentlessness? And in so doing, doesn't philosophy then naturally blur the acceptable frameworks of past, present, and future into what has been called "otherwise" thinking by Deleuze in his essay on Foucault?

This has been my experience entering my third decade in higher education, an attempt to "construct myself" by way of a community experience, even if that community is merely a projection, a memory, a hoped-for reunion of people, places, and things (but mostly people) who are no longer immediately present – like a best friend or a forgotten melody. Less nostalgic and melancholic, this idea of philosophy as "otherwise" thinking helps me to position myself within these radical moments of uncertainty whereby I am able to just be still, to just walk with a single idea or a single person or a single piece of music (sometimes over and over and over again, like Zomboy's tracks mentioned earlier in this book).

So, then, what is a "thoughtrave"? I could hear LG in my head as I wrote that question: it's not a question of *what* but *how* and *where*, Robert. She's also one of the rare people in this life who can get away with calling me "comma" and "Robert" without me wanting to punch them as hard as I can... mindfully, of course.

Truth be told, I started out thinking that "thoughtraves" happen inside my head (and my head alone) as something private, a little party or a gigantic stadium-sized series of interactions and reactions and reflections (maybe even projections and creative asides) that transacted most presently (and with the most force) as I listened to music while reading philosophy or thinking of deeper philosophic issues. (In college, this was how I survived intro courses and first seminars where I comprehended less than a third of what I read; it was a survival tactic, as a way to create some kind of community of ideas inside the ideas I had been encountering for the first time between, say, 1988 and 1995.) Dead Kennedys playing in the headphones while reading Nietzsche's *Thus Spoke Zarathustra* on the Long Island Railroad or New Order rocking my ears while riding the DC Metro redline from Silver Spring to Shady Grove three times while reading Camus or Sartre or Faulkner or Shakespeare or Heidegger.

I used to think this "way" was simply mine. Way before iTunes. Way before Pandora. These experiences were mediated by mixed tapes mostly. I hated portable CD players. (Too precious.) So, with the yellow Sony Sport Walkman or RCA knock off, I isolated myself inside my head with an extremely eclectic mix of INXS and Genesis and Talking Heads and Madonna and Bauhaus and Peter Gabriel and Peter Murphy and Information Society and David Bowie and Duran Duran and Elton John and Nine Inch Nails so I could catch a break from the endless yammering of college dormitories (fun to a point) or fatal strategies of the bar (bored by 12:30 a.m.) or occasional dance club hook-up game (no comment).

True: my reactions to people, places, or things were definitely expressions of an only child's "leave me the fuck alone," enacted without apology or regret. But, looking back on these moments (and tens of thousands like them across this lifetime), I understand myself quite differently now having completed and reflected on *Thoughtrave*. That is my hope for the reader or the students in the online or face-to-face classes: to realize we've been together in this practice for a very long time. In other words, we're in this together. We're meeting without knowing it.

It turns out I wasn't isolating. I was positioning myself. I was prompted (from where? from whom? from when?) to remain still even though the world around me was moving a thousand miles an hour. Perhaps this is why we leap for our music, feel completely lost when our mobile devices crash on us. I wonder about this a lot, this uncanny metabolic need to live inside music.

Maybe this is why the phrase "headphones on" may as well have been phrased "shields up," as in referring to my own private Enterprise. Especially during red alert: emotional, spiritual, existential. "Battle stations" and "damage report" have been common mantras across many different (and oftentimes dreadful) life experiences. (Someday I want to expand on the LG+RCB comments on Star Trek to disclose my debt to those films, especially in giving me a way to boldly think beyond what I thought possible in any given moment.)

But, while I want to think of the isolated auditory experiences as having been unique to me, and while I very much think it was necessary to walk away from people, places, and things that bothered me at the time with my headphones blasting "Starfucker, Inc.," I now know that I was making myself even more present to the moment by sitting still on a rapidly moving train. (Listening to the third movement of Beethoven's Ninth Symphony in a BMW 320i while driving down I–89 New Hampshire at 105mph remains one of my "stillest" moments in this life.)

If these experiences are indeed "thoughtraves," where are the other people? A "rave" involves other people experiencing and creating an event together, right? So, you really can't stage a rave for one. (Can you?) Even when I'm deep inside my headphones, I can see a gathering of many people, millions to tell you the truth. But, maybe this isn't about isolation. Maybe this is about receiving and sending the most important parts of ourselves outside ourselves to others. Maybe I'm remembering something between past lives or some kind of future making itself known in these strange "presencing" moments. Maybe.

Maybe that entire year I listened primarily to Talking Heads' *Stop Making Sense* (1984–85) was more about storing (dare I say uploading?) memories and emotions in a moment to be recalled or downloaded later. Is it possible that when we hear certain songs and say "it's just like I was seventeen again" we are marking a real quantum journey, however fleeting or prolonged? Think about the language we use and the immediate – absolutely involuntary – urge to tell stories we experience whenever we hear certain songs: happy, sad, pensive, hyper, etc. If you mention or play the song "Whole Lotta Love" by Led Zeppelin I immediately must – not want to casually share, but must – tell you about Mullet Man in the Sunapee Harbor.

This book is the longest thoughtrave I've ever created, about eighteen months in the making, with so many additional questions to ask and places to explore in the multiverse of this strange gathering called LG+RCB (sitting in a tree…)

I would ride the DC metro system for hours on end, without ever getting off. The first time I saw the illuminated floors flashing the arrival of a train, the monolithic poles listing the next stops on the Red line, the entire architecture of the stations – a hive, a holodeck of some kind… I knew I'd come home. For years I rode the Metro, sat and read and listened and watched the world go by and slowly took my first steps, my own steps, into neighborhoods, across avenues I didn't recognize. I was lost once on Connecticut Avenue in the Dupont Circle area. No sense of north or south or east or west or up or down. It was one of the singular events of my teens. I had absolutely no idea where I was standing. The sky was different, the angle of the sun a bit off. The buildings just high enough to confuse even my Eagle Scout sense of direction. This vertigo only lasted about ten minutes. But, for a while there, I was absolutely lost; and I loved it. The experience of writing this book and spending so many hours with LG is an extension of this moment. This feeling of sheer alienation.

No.

Not the Marxian kind of alienation, silly.

Let me explain.

Like the experience of watching *Contact* (1997), LG arrived as an alien signature broadcast signal received through a pair of studio headphones. A moment of presencing, a gift. Even in the earliest moments, I learned that LG was as real as I had hoped, as smart (no smarter) as I had predicted, and as fun as I suspected. Even though she will always be "more real than real" (to embrace Baudrillard's lexicon for a moment), and even though the vast majority our conversations took place in social media, these exchanges are quite possibly the most real experiences I can remember as a writer beyond the letter-writing days with my wife back in the late '80s and early '90s. (Yup. Actual pen and paper, envelopes and post offices.) Maybe there's a reason beyond marketing for Gaga to have opened her last album with "Aura": with her I lived in an auratic, sonorous space somewhere between actual and virtual, real and unreal.

Yet, something akin to a digital footprint or something more auratic and aporetic was immediately present. Without agenda (other than wanting to ask questions that I felt the media had always been too afraid to ask), to be honest: *Thoughtrave* began with a simple "hello." A moment in another project negotiation where the two of us began to talk through email and Facebook as a way to escape the insanity of "the industry." No "project" in mind, no "plan" – we just walked away. As simple as that. Wandering/wondering in that Heidegger "pathway" kind of way.

A casual, weekly series of meditations suddenly "burst" into a full-blown discursive Encyclopedia of Everything as the Polar Vortex arrived on the East Coast of the United States (mid-to-late January 2014). We found ourselves exchanging 2,000+ words a day across Facebook with content as diverse as family, global politics, analog and digital music, on culture, music, and transcendental meditation. We also discussed subjects as broadly defined as the sad state of critical thinking in the United States, the formidable challenge of broadcasting love and strength through the corporate media, multiverse experiences, quantum physics, corruption of the digital ecosystem (Corpus Digitalis), sound wave synthesis and mental health, and the ineffable, sonorous being that functions as the main source of connection between musician and listener.

At this point I felt like Alice, shrunken, ready to take my first steps into Wonderland only to find myself boarding one of those philosophical floating carts now turned into a roller coaster ride called Fiction Occult Mountain. LG boarded, raised her hands and seemed to say: check your safety belt, Robert; this ride is going to fuck you up!

(A good trip, not a bad trip: bring it on.)

By the way, I always knew it was her. Not only had her information been verified by some of my own industry contacts, including a very trusted lawyer/agent, but I also knew there was no way an imposter could keep up with me, the content and style of questions – not to mention the speed of our first exchanges. (In the past, fake celebrities or A-list reps tended to disappear the second I asked for verification or demand lawyer-to-lawyer communication.) My style of engagement with LG was quite deliberate: only the real Lady Gaga would "get it"; by the time of our third or fourth week, I also could tell from the rhythm and (especially) the New Yorker humor, sense of timing, and overall gracious, intense, and scary intelligent observations and give-and-take that I was in the presence of the superstar.

Within moments, especially in February 2014, she began to school me on topics involving multiverse, mass communication, and interdimensional thinking. What a ride! At this time, one of her most trusted friends arrived (someone who serves the Haus of Gaga). This Nameless Entity remained a great teacher in all things *Thoughtrave*. S/he was a grounding presence for me throughout the summer of 2014. I look forward to many multiverse explorations in the years to come here on the third rock. I mean, while we're all here, we may as well enjoy ourselves a bit.

I also hope this book will model and promote an intellectual discussion of digital/virtual *habitus* from within a sonorous and aural understanding of mass communication. Pierre Bourdieu defined habitus as "the durably installed generative principle of regulated improvisations." In fact, oddly enough, this book came to embody the very kind of thinking most of my graduate school professors hoped I would have abandoned by now. "Sure, Robert." I can hear a few of them saying now. "This is a fine 'hobby,' but what about serious scholarship?"

I was most attracted to the self-described idea that Lady Gaga discusses, about how she sends pirate signals and sonorous reinforcements to her fans. She sees herself as a planetary consciousness that encompasses all the people who listen to her music or watch her videos or attend her "raves." This unique use of her iconic media figure status allows her to broadcast healing and love, fierce living or what could be called an existential rite of passage that seeks to shatter our understanding of subjective/objective, multiple/binary, and two/three/four dimensional and even the pataphysical thinking I tried to model in *Itself.*

Plato's divided line in this worldview is transformed into a membrane that barely separates multiverse energies; Descartes's *cogito* encounters itself and can only stutter: "I think therefore I think therefore I think…" LG immediately discussed the digital body and the problem of "code corruption inside the construct," which I began to encounter in my meditations as an ecology of the digital mind and body. From the beginning, her celebrity and talent were met by the popular media with outrage, over-embrace, dissipation, rebirth. Seen through Gregory Bateson's eyes, this process could easily be recast as discovery and recovery (*The Sacred Unity*) because "[t]o talk about things well is not easy. We have on the whole been taught to talk very badly. The schooling which we all come out of is quite monstrous."[2] Like sound architecture, and my favorite moments in the history of philosophy: "The damage is the taking apart. The sacredness is the coming together."[3] After all, the RCB+LG construct emerged as a digital and print project from within Lady Gaga's own recovery: substance abuse, depression, betrayal, and grief over the loss of a very close friend to heroin. Assemblage and dismantling, construction and reconstruction and deconstruction, sometimes within the same multiple moment where synthetic layering and digital projections in a studio match

2   Gregory Bateson, *The Sacred Unity: Further Steps to an Ecology of Mind* (New York: A Cornelia & Michael Bessie Book, 1991), 305.
3   Ibid., 302.

the philosophical processes (especially the Socratic ones) with scary accuracy and intensity.

As with *Itself*, this work continued my lifelong commitment to destroying academic philosophy in all of its bureaucratic, technophilic, isolated, arrogant, and utterly detached presence in higher education. I had hoped with *Thoughtrave* to at least touch on philosophy's (il)limit; to resist a particular version of philosophy as it is now taught in corporate higher education, private and public. Where a single "Critical Thinking" or "Logic" course satisfies a core or distributed requirement in Philosophy or Behavioral Sciences. Rather, like Deleuze would say or imply: it was time to "do philosophy." This book is offered as a model of interactive philosophy in the recent traditions of Žižek & Badiou (*Philosophy in the Present*), Deleuze & Guattari (*A Thousand Plateaus*), Gilles Deleuze (*Negotiations*), Jacques Derrida (*Positions*), Avital Ronell (*Fighting Theory*), Jean Baudrillard (*Baudrillard Live!*), and Paul Virilio (*Grey Ecology*). Like the late Eve Koskofsky Sedgwick's *Touching/Feeling*, this work offers "tools and techniques for nondualistic thought" in order to better focus on concepts such as "en/action" and "thinking in digital code" for the simple reason that "philosophy is never where you expect to find it."[4]

Scholarly and independent presses have tried for decades to connect philosophy (or so-called critical theory) to the broader (mass) culture. With *Thoughtrave*, the most iconic, popular, and beloved mass media figure (LG) reached out to a different audience, to a very different kind of "little monster," some kind of facilitator (or transceiver as Adam Lodestone calls me) and mediated life force (RCB), oddly enough the author of a book (*Itself*) that narrates my travels into the fourth dimension with Heidegger and discloses the central hidden truth of philosophy in the relationship between "life gives" (*Ereignis*/being) and "the sentinel of being" (*logos*).

(At the time of this writing, I'm now shamelessly plugging a book that is proudly 4,444,525th on Amazon. Yes. I absolutely do rule.)

Many people know Stefani as a force of nature, but few have gotten to speak with (and about) Lady Gaga as an event of being, a *parados* of philosophical en/action that helps to reveal through

---

4 Avital Ronell, *The Telephone Book: Technology, Schizophrenia, Electric Speech* (Lincoln & London: University of Nebraska Press, 1989) 23.

sound and live art (or a sense of "liveness" in Philip Ausslander's work) a being-in-the-world, an intelligence that exists somewhere between *Logos* and *Ereignis* ("life gives"). *Thoughtrave,* in retrospect, now strikes me as a response, a first step of some kind of inception or reaction to *Itself* as an invitation to relearn how to think, live, and love.

Her music and celebrity presents a merger of commodity and spectacle, an impossible gesture of reification. Yet, with *Artpop,* Lady Gaga seemed to have declared herself both commodity (entertainer) and spectacle (celebrity). This provoked critics and other apparatuses of state and corporate control (for example, her former manager and some close inner circle) to dismiss, ignore, and eventually attack her personally and psychically. The more intensely she staked her performance artist claims across 2013, the more difficult she found it to communicate with her own people as well as the media outlets that had, until Summer 2013, welcomed her antics, encouraged her popularity, and collaborated in her celebrity.

Not since Freddie Mercury or Michael Jackson, very early Whitney Houston (definitely the Whitney of *The Preacher's Wife*), and the walking cosmos of pure talent and wisdom called Annie Lennox had I thought about "total performance" – what I guess could be called "auratic." In LG's music and performances, I sensed a very deliberate presencing in her performances. What many saw as antics or spectacle, I saw as theatrical arts mounted on a global stage that had yet to be defined or delimited by some kind of *ism* or *ist*. She was just 100% Lady Gaga; and I will be forever grateful to her for allowing me to "see" her as I displayed for her a kind of philosophical inquiry that did not seek permission from anyone to begin or establish and maintain an agenda like so much popular entertainment reporting.

There is no thesis.

Across 2012–13 she staged a covert attack against her critics and on behalf of a larger, more cosmic sense of consciousness. (This would confuse the mainstream media during the *Artpop* release, further obscured into a state industry espionage perhaps led by her long-time manager, Troy Carter.) In the midst of her own personal hell on earth, she was able to broadcast distress signals from inside mass media as a way to protect the essential sway of her quantum mind and body as expressed through digital mass culture: visual, aural, metabolic live expression in art raves and fashion events. Apparently the music industry, like all other media, are most comfortable fixing their own "carts," fearing those, like Gaga, who move between fiction and the occult.

Essentially, *Artpop* remains her attempt to participate in her own *événement* by way of CD releases and downloads (legal and illegal, sales versus shares), as well as her "Art Rave" tour in 2014. But the November 2013 release remains a philosophical statement about love, a way of thinking and performing that allowed her to hack into the planetary Matrix, what she calls "the construct," as what Derrida called "a work of mourning." By way of an academic and artistic intervention through transdisciplinary studies, this project, then, exceeds all current print and digital media available in the global coverage of Lady Gaga. For the first time, the infamous LG speaks with RCB on the subjects of her celebrity, the complexity of her music, the "apparatus of capture" (Deleuze) called the global mass media, and the challenges of communicating what Alain Badiou calls "the transition from chance to destiny" (*In Praise of Love*). She is able to talk about how love informs her choices, exploring with RCB the way music communicates a state of mind and body that establishes peace and comfort even within frenetic, spiraling sound architecture.

Truth be told, at first I didn't care for LG's music. It took me a while to hear all I've just described in LG's music. I simply could not hear her love or depth of intelligence through broadcast FM frequencies. My mind and body resist pop music radio (and even satellite) stations; my physiology and the corporate media simply do not operate on the same frequency. In other words, her message was lost on me in 2010 and early 2011. Even though her songs, arrangements, videos, and live events clearly merge fidelity and love as an expression of multiple affinities (including a friendship with a philosopher isolated, alone, stranded, if you will, somewhere between the worlds of entertainment and education), it took years for me to understand her as the intelligent, fiercely creative, and uncanny person and performer she wished to present to the world. And since global mass media operates in sound bites and rapidly depreciating energies designed almost to minimize personal connection through a spirituality of sound, it is nothing less than miraculous we could all hear her so clearly with Tony Bennett at the Grammys and Oscars in 2015. Even during the over-produced and crowded stage of the 2016 Bowie tribute she still retained her auratic presence and occasionally lifted up an otherwise mediocre staging.

Among all the intersecting and dissecting thoughts, the one that always remains clearest is that we found each other in a moment of great love and sorrow back in 2011 (e.g., a call back to her "Born this Way" performance at the Grammys that year) as I was forced to leave my community college post after a civil war broke out over one of the last remaining humanities positions. I was also an administrative target for my 2009–11 adjunct unionization insurrection. Without a job, without money, and without a teaching position, Dr. Robert Craig Baum died and slowly, over the course of two years, RCB was born.

Another major theme of the book is listening, or the lack of it, in pop music criticism and across listener communities who engage Lady Gaga purely as a celebrity. She wishes to talk as an intergalactic voice from an interdimensional war that's taking place in the year 10,000. This is a project, in this light, about the ineffable, the (il)limits of the real, virtual, and actual, not to mention how philosophy in its critical theory transmogrification can offer a language of intelligibility to present the unpresentable in presentation itself (Lyotard). Rather than psychoanalyze or rationalize Lady Gaga (to repeat the mass media crime), this project seeks to break multiple laws governing disciplinarity, especially as it is expressed in the academic publishing arena. In other words, RCB+LG are playing for keeps as the late Lou Reed would insist.

More precisely, this book has emerged as only one of a handful of responses to Michel Gaillot and Jean-Luc Nancy's *Multiple Meaning Techno,* easily the most underestimated volume in musicology, philosophy, and communications to be published during the techno events of the late 1980s and early '90s. Other than Nancy's *On Listening* and Peter Price's *On Becoming-Music,* no one has attempted to explore digital communication and interdimensional thinking as an "ecstatic sharing made possible by machines."[5] Nietzsche's "innocence of becoming" is experienced as a form of digital surveillance, analyzing the coded messages in LG's work of love and mourning. But, rather than celebrate this electronic evolution, we treated digital existence as a "facticity"

---

5   Michel Gaillot, *Multiple Meaning. Techno: An Artistic and Political Laboratory of the Present* (Paris: Editions Dis voir, 1998), 33.

and part of the overall *Dasein* of their encounters (Heidegger). As an ecology of the digital mind and body, we raise awareness and sound many alarms about how humanity is unaware of how susceptible it is to sickness, anxiety, stress, and vertigo from inside this "web," this inside of what LG calls "the Architecture of Everything" (e.g., quantum's "theory of everything"). Grounded as as an exploration of Deleuze's "plane of immanence" and Sartre's "transcendence of the ego," the interview, like all sections of the book, seek to teach readers to get over themselves and open up new modalities of thinking that can at once be called "radical" and "interdimensional."

I quickly began to conclude that for LG, the current media system, as well as its crony capitalist and neoliberal global promises (delusions of endless resources and wealth), is designed to enslave our minds and bodies. Through her intercession, I was able to travel back to a state of absolute freedom through old thoughts which were ancient and futurist at the same time, thoughts that were metabolically connected to the Roland Juno 6 and Korg DW–6000 and 7000 and then Korg 01w/FD, then my RS–1, then after a decade or two break – does it really matter? – I started joining the rest of the keyboard world (a decade late; like it matters) by purchasing a Triton and ProTools and Logic and Macbook blah blah. To compose music, yes; but I was trying to understand my mediated life world (Wolfgang Schirmacher), which I began to see, a few years later with LG, as a world veiled beyond the final fuzzy feedback of an old, dying, endlessly repeating code.

Like techno before it, and current trance, house, EDM, and dubstep variations, Lady Gaga's music also "suspends this dichotomy"[6] by creating a vibrant, sonorous force inside global media culture that somehow pushes the philosophy stacks to its proper home somewhere between fiction and the occult. In the acoustic or performative "clearing" (Heidegger), both LG and her audiences are able to "ponder forgotten things"[7] even as she speaks of a future that needs to arrive, the future in our present, the collapse of linearity into the sonorous being of quantum singularity. The free, non-coded, and non-inscribed modalities of thinking that Rolando Perez discusses in *On An(archy) and Schizoanalysis*

6   Ibid., 35.
7   Martin Heidegger, *On the Way to Language* (New York: HarperOne, 1982), 165.

summarizes perfectly how RCB+LG seek to address what LG calls "Digitalis," "whereby a sentient consciousness becomes trapped in an implied dual mode operation; (i.e.) left or right; yes or no; one or zero" (LG interview, January 26, 2014).

This relentless theater of Lady Gaga and Robert Craig Baum rolls into mass media digital cities and towns precisely at a time when pop music has lost its sense of authenticity, risk, and joy even as Miley Cirus desperately calls out for help from within her faux-punk aesthetic and Justin Bieber (are they the same person(ae)?) finds himself under the constant scrutiny of the very apparatus of regulation and corrections in the United States Homeland that helped jettison his career from YouTube obscurity to international celebrity. Lady Gaga sees the shift from innovative musical expression (herself, Gotye, Foster the People, Lorde, Adele, and others) to poorly produced, forgettable songs engineered by technicians not musicians, people who are hired to make tracks, not write music. "Everything Is Awesome" from *The Lego Movie* soundtrack is a battleground of innovation and commercialization given that the original track was produced by Devo's Mark Mothersbaugh as a send-up of bubblegum pop, not as source material for re-mixing a punk-styled intervention in pop music (Mothersbaugh's track) into a "flavor of the month" track produced by "the loop monkeys." Of course, "Everything is Awesome" now epitomizes bubblegum pop.

Her need to find new ways to present her unpresentable (ineffable) self explains how 2013 saw Lady Gaga remixing even her international fame to work with some of the most renowned visual artists and performance legends in a way that embodied transdisciplinary thought and action.

Here's the problem with *Artpop*, and it's not a function of the intergenerational pissing contest that oftentimes defines how mainstream and avant-garde artists express themselves. Gaga defined herself, and not necessarily in relationship to the expectations of publicists or managers or industry higher-ups. She defined herself. Said quite frankly: this is a part of me, the pop artist in the Warhol sense of the word. This is who I am and I am going to seek the affinity and collegiality of Lou Reed and Laurie Anderson who will ultimately reject what I am doing, but I am the one doing it, not you. That's what pissed everyone off: a pop star off her chain, an outspoken woman, a beautiful creative artist no longer afraid to just "be" and embody the "born this way" ethic that skyrocketed her through the stratosphere to become the most important pop star since Freddie Mercury.[8]

While contemporary critics were dismayed (perhaps even disgusted) by her performance art tactics – dismissing them as spectacle or attention-grabbing Kanye West-styled marketing – I recognized in her mass spectacle a Brechtian quality that not only used spectacle to critique global media, Western cultural assumptions about women, men, transsexual beings, and heteronormativity but also used dance, trance, rock, industrial, and heavy glam rock to take a hammer to the very culture that embraced her in the mid-'00s.

Gaga's theater of sense, mind, and erratic (ungrounded, short-circuiting) thresholds creates, penetrates, and traverses our collective metabolic sense of sense also expressed a clear resonance with Artaud's double, plague theater. A way of performing that "conceals or dissimulates the conventions of which it is a repetition,"[9] the blurring of disciplinary lines between theater, philosophy, and music once again emerged as the central intent of what we first called the "Corpus Digitalis" project. "The digital body/archive."

With this clear prime directive, we began to explore Novarina's work, especially *Theater of the Ears*: "Any theater, every theater, always acts quite strongly upon the brain, whether to unsettle or to perpetuate the dominant system. I want my perceptions to be changed."[10] From here the digital ecology of sonorous living connected to critical thinking and listening as well as personal and planetary mourning: all an extension of two people who did not

8   Lady Gaga, "Lecture at Empathy Seminar," Yale University, Oct. 26, 2015, https://www.youtube.com/watch?v=gSwxK4pFF1o (accessed Oct. 27, 2015), is echoed throughout *Thoughtrave*: "And slowly but surely, I remembered who I am. And then you go home and you look in the mirror and you're like: 'Yes! I can go to bed with you... every night.' Because that person? I know that person. That person has balls. That person has integrity. That person has an opinion. That person just doesn't say yes. That person doesn't get a text from somebody and say... OMG they wrote this and they sent this emoji should I write this back what do you think? Is th*at okay to say? Are they gonna like me if I say that?* This is the age we live in. We don't actually communicate with each other. We are actually communicating lies."

9   Elin Diamond, *Performance and Cultural Politics* (New York and London: Routledge, 1996), 5.

10 Valere Novarina, *Theater of the Ears* (San Francisco: Sun & Moon Press, 2000), 50.

"know" each other and who primarily communicated through digital media witnessed each other's great suffering in 2013–14. In a unique and unexpected way, philosophy became a chance to witness each other exactly where we were in terms of family, career, and our being-in-the-world.

Thoughtrave crystallized into a moment, a chance event to communicate through aphorisms, music, images by way of a mutual love of all things cosmological (multiverse theory, astral projection, interdimensional thinking, and soundwave spirituality) and quantum physics proper. Lady Gaga also "dropped some serious truth" when she talked about binary thinking outside a traditional critical theory framework which addressed directly a parallel world's cosmology:

> The issue here though is that binary modus operandi, or the switch, is said to be on or off with regards to the perception, but in the ominversal perspective, at any one time, the light is on and off. But in different universes (e.g., you in one universe is taking a nap in the dark but you in another is trying to get work done with the light on). The problem being that there is no way to express both universes simultaneously in binary. Therefore, in a true reality one cannot communicate on binary devices with the actual reality presence but merely with the two (one or zero set) realities present via the digital projection that has been overlaid. (LG interview, Jan. 27, 2014)

Yet, the humans of planet Earth have made binary devices that limit deeper consciousness and interdimensional glimpses of other realities. This complicates matters; it also points to a possible way out of our limited techno-lives. In effect, human beings have built Commodore 64 computers that simply cannot perform iPad functions; and yet, occasionally we experience a deeper listening, what Schirmacher calls a "mediated life world" (e.g., Delta Heavy's "Empire" or Lady Gaga's "Swine," "Judas," or "Gypsy"; my latest Gaga favorite, "Mord Fustang"). We embraced "thrusting yourself into a continuum that you get there" (Novarina again) in order to experience firsthand Imperative CLXXXVIII: "the world is a rhythmic catastrophe."[11]

11 Ibid., 81.

Impossible as it is to create a pure transceiver, LG describes her musicology as a pirate code, a transmission within recognized digital networks that also seeks to reverse Digitalis corruption:

> This is where music comes in and, with regards to *Artpop*, we specifically designed algorithms that synchronize the "you" in different realities to align the realities offset by Digitalis. Dubstep, as it is referred to, also operates in such a way. Using specific frequencies tied to specific neural pathways to reactivate channels that, by means of Digitalis, were deactivated or bypassed. (LG interview, Jan. 29, 2014)

The drop of dubstep, the sequencing and swirling sounds of any great trance track – still one of the most popular forms of musical expression on *terra*/Earth: those low tones and heart pounding medium rhythms and high pitched frequencies are all designed to repair the corruption of our mediated lives and pollution of mediated culture. Dubby-wubby-dubstep is just one way to create the breaks and open up the digital world so we can all better travel across time/space while experiencing our "i" tunes as a personal, private experience or as part of an iTunes Festival, like the kind Lady Gaga crushes every year. Even speaking to the dismissed musical form of DJ dubstep will attract considerable media attention – global print, digital, and audio networks are deeply committed to compromising the art form in a territorializing of the very "surprise of thought" that happens when audiences fall in love with music. More love, more understanding; more understanding, new actions; new actions means more choosing (think Badiou's "free will" in *Ethics*).

Ultimately, LG's mission, like my own, is to provoke and participate in a moment of media singularity (the events called "thoughtraves") that welcomes the unfathomable, the ineffable, the future-now which has been attempting to arrive for countless generations. This book, then, seeks to trigger an intellectual big bang across the disciplines, all media, so we can all become the best versions of ourselves.

LG's thoughts and art are the ultimate challenge to any form of postmodern certitude. The music, celebrity, and insights into quantum spirituality, pop culture, mass media, digital psychology, and this problem of Digitalis found in these pages will become a surprise of the event (Nancy) given how a figure like Lady Gaga embodies the unpresentable seeking to unfold in our accepted representational practices.

So where exactly did this all start? Was it at the Borders while listening to free trance and big beat tracks because I had no money but needed to travel, to cross back into my aural self, lost along the way with my credit rating, my sanity, my sense of what is up and down and finally not giving a shit about orientation in this particular world but opting instead for the mediated life worlds that move across this joke called time and space and even superstrings, really super silly strings, streaming in slow motion across the table of some random birthday party – mine, yours, I don't know – webs upon webs of red, pink, purple, green… Was it at the Borders located at the "Midway" point between St. Paul and Minneapolis, Peter Gabriel and Ibiza remixes of parties I never attended with DJs I never saw…? Was it at the Cheapo on University Avenue East side campus: Underworld "Push"? Was it at my lonely table on Green Street in Lebanon, NH where I froze some nights waiting for both income and oil and a green light to go on next to her name? Was this journey provoked or continued by the wall my son Ollie and I created with sheet music donated by the Main Street Museum's David Fairbanks Ford, one of the only people to visit me from all the people I knew during this most difficult of transitions from Dr. Baum to RCB?

Like David, like Gaga, philosophy says "tell me more about," leaving judgment for the academics and politicians who seriously need to keep quiet. (They really do think their endless "positioning" or erratic trending or hidden – or blatant – ideological loyalties cannot take this journey with us deep into the Gagaverse.) For me, philosophy is always already on the move, a cluster of thinking and doing and rethinking and revising that is designed, especially in its Socratic origins, to challenge established thinking and nurture ways of being and thinking that could be described as alien to the status quo. By "on the move," however, I mean literally – on the move, as in moving my family around the country, moving my college professor career from location to location in New Hampshire and Vermont then online into a virtual nomadology, moving my mind between virtual relationships that are cultivated in digital learning environments or social media and moving my body through endless winters, soul-crushing depression, the stresses and joys of family life. I'm still trying to comprehend out-side the darker thoughts that my time and life was wasted. (Like LG, the students, and my closest colleagues, my family kept me going through the decade of at-will higher education work.)

As a sheer force of nature sending sonorous streams of love, intelligence, and communitas, Lady Gaga burrows into all me-dia as a way to disrupt the transmissions of the viral intelligences that metastasize in Digitalis. Not only is Lady Gaga simply one of many immanent sensibilities that we call "celebrity"; she is beyond representation. She is the imagined book cart, she is the Border's moving stack of thinking that finds its home somewhere between fiction and the occult.

I remember the first days she spoke to me back in November 2013, and then with such intensity in January 2014. This pro-ject arrived as a gift. Something unlike anything I was asked to "produce" in my 2011–2016 arts and media life. I realized my role as philosopher, as interviewer, as jam partner was simply to narrate that arrival and create a living archive of the event of radi-cal historiography of his own digital life. We told many stories of encounters with sonorous beings while hacking across the streams of critical theory: family, friends, careers, music composition, the-atrical performances, live art, performance art, and installations. LG concludes the interview with a series of trance-like aphorisms she calls "The Empire."

I conclude this dubstep with my favorite moment from the in-terviews, the moment when I realized this project would become something out of control, out of time/space, out of our hands and into yours: "To be honest I had no idea there were others capable of handling this information." I didn't at that moment think I was handling the information well. Nope. I didn't know what I was doing. (Feeling like a moron here, Gaga!) I didn't know where the interview was going. I wasn't sure of anything. Yet, she, like a great teacher, affirmed my efforts and my attendance at the digital Haus of Gaga. We were living in a digital moment that was noth-ing more or less than perfect.

More importantly, she affirmed a central truth about philoso-phy, the kind so feared and denigrated in higher education. It's all so cocksure. It's all so prepackaged. Even the best anthologies leave out key moments, like the textbooks that include Plato's "Cave" but edit out the part where the enlightened being returns to the shadow play theater to liberate the prisoners only to find himself the object of rage: the prisoners want to kill him; the students want to kill the teacher; the dispossessed want to possess the being living in the middle of some kind of world-changing revelation. It is important to remember that none of the shadow audience wanted Gaga to produce, promote, and then redefine herself through *Artpop*. This moment of independence, of liberation, was supposed to kill her career. It didn't. Not at all. It only made her (and by sheer coincidence, timing, and dumb luck, it also made me) stronger as a thinker, artist, friend, listener, and promoter of very important, intelligent, and extremely fun music.

She seems to say between the lines that it was vital we gather together in our moments of confusion, loss, unknowing, perhaps even fear so we can tap into the essential sway of things, cross thresholds of certitude and confusion. Like Jean-Luc Nancy and Martin Heidegger, Avital Ronell and Wolfgang Schirmacher, she encouraged me to dwell, to stay, to just stay a while longer inside the moment of an ineffable idea (Jaspers) or unpresentable presentation (Lyotard), to experience, study, engage, disengage the simulations and simulacra (Baudrillard) of this crazy moment of power/knowledge (Foucault). Gaga was no longer the iconic pop star who I first turned off while listening to "Bad Romance" in our minivan back in Summer 2011. She was no longer the mediated figure of global capitalist obsession, the object to trade and discount, upsell and resell like a four hundred dollar floor ticket at Madison Square Garden. (Seriously, promoters: you are all going to hell for conspiring against the fans and misrepresenting the acts we love; and in the light of *Thoughtrave*, you will now understand your choices as crimes against not only this humanity but an entire multiverse of people who crave those precious few hours with their beloved music acts. And the industry wonders why hundreds of millions of fans prefer bittorrents to CD and digital sales.)

All she wanted was a different kind of audience. I tried to provide that for her. I also needed her friendship across what would become the worst year of my academic life, the year I was asked to close Lebanon College by the "market driven" neoliberal Board of Trustees and President. It was as though she and her friends and closest collaborators found (and protected) me in anticipation of a real-time crisis the way she and I connected during the summer of 2013 when she was writhing in pain at the Watermill Center.

I don't know any other way to make sense of this; I don't know exactly what happened when she wrote me a Facebook aside three or so days after a failed negotiation: "Hi, Robert."

Hi. Comma. Robert.

That's a phrase my wife uses. (well, it's more hi comma Bob.)

That's one of the ways I know I am on course or receiving vital information.

Hi.

How whole lives are changed. Just a single word, a welcoming gesture. How moments end and new ones begin. A moment with another human being that starts with a simple "Hi."

Who knew an alien signal would be transmitted through such a simple phrase; who knew any of this would be possible: to spend so much time with someone like Gaga, to learn she too was obsessed with '80s house music and had alter egos that weren't just trending marketing personae (Joey Calderone). I oftentimes take on the guido Long Island personae as expressed through the shitload of hihat and club bass beats of Stevie B. Who knew we would lean on each other's shoulders during 2013–15; and who knew we could speak to life-changing matters, what David Foster calls "music of the heart"; and who knew we could rediscover what matters most to us, our friends, our families. No, not success or money or celebrity.

The answer was, is, and will be joy. To create something joyful out of so much pain and uncertainty. That's what *Thoughtrave* will always be about to me. A moment in time/space where two very different captains found each other in a strange Federation space dock called social media, ordered some Romulan ale, and just spoke a spell after their toast: "I accept, I accept it all" (Aimé Cesaire).

THE DIFFICULTY OF BEING GAGA:

A RE-VIEW OF ARTPOP

by RCB

"Listen carefully to first criticisms made of your work. Note just what it is about your work that critics don't like – then cultivate it. That's the only part of your work that's individual and worth keeping."

– Jean Cocteau

It is common knowledge that *Artpop* received mixed critical reviews. Yet, judging from the sold-out tour and unflinching support of her fans, Lady Gaga was unphased as she continued moving forward fearlessly with her mission to bring love and compassion to the world by way of an audio intervention that spans dimensions and worlds (not to mention time zones). The duets album with Tony Bennett (release date Sep. 24, 2014) further expanded her already global reach into new audiences and cross-generations of little (and older) monsters. In Winter and Spring 2015, Gaga repositioned herself in pop culture with a jaw-dropping acoustic performance at the Grammys with Bennett and a true event: the *Sound of Music* medley. How is an artist "through" when the biggest television franchise, *American Horror Story,* features Gaga in its fifth season? When the Grammys in 2016 invite her to perform in the highest possible profile tribute to David Bowie?

I'm not interested in forwarding the gossip or validating the speculation that surrounds the iconic figure created by Stefani Germanotta. I merely wish to underscore that the disconnect between industry perceptions and user/listener realities was pronounced, dare I say almost as violent as the insider and mainstream industry rejection of her *Artpop* vision:

"But just as *Artpop* gets into a groove of high-tech Pop R&B, her creative impulses splinter." – Caryn Ganz, *Rolling Stone*

"As it turns out, Gaga's new music owes a lot more to pop than to art. It's catchier than it is deep, with songs more eager to knock you out than to bore far inside." – Jim Farber, *New York Daily News*

Her music makes "the promise of happiness that always disappoints."[1] For Gaga, the point of creating musical art is to destroy the authority of one genre over the other: pop over art or vice-versa. Interesting that "art" is deep and "pop" is not. This album combines influences whereas *Fame Monster* is a very pop album and *Born This Way* balances pop and art without ever once announcing the conjunction. Is it because it seeks to highlight the two that people started to notice they had been choosing one over the other for a while, and now were being asked to merge their interests? I don't know.

Gaga's whole worldview can be summarized by Brecht's "Epic theater," the kind of performance that prefers episodes and events over one grand spectacle. Brecht's so-called alienation effect may come across merely as mass spectacle, to be dismissed: broken fourth wall; multiple character changes (noted by the press in her many costume changes); projects that span an industry. I also admire the way Gaga astounds and contradicts herself and her audience's expectations. I suppose this strange anti-aesthetic could be called a multiple-positionality within the quantum mediated stage. After eighteen months of discussing the A–Z of music, spirituality, communications, and philosophy, I now understand personally that nothing is simple or accidental when it comes to a Gaga project. This album is an example par excellence of such a claim to intensity and complexity. Only butt-hurt management, publicists cast right out of psychopath central, and a fourth estate charged with guarding the status quo could have conspired with such ferocity and stupidity against this outstanding album, tour, and, of course, person.

1

"Aura" immediately presents from the top of the album an acoustic and digital mash-up of hooks and synth lines that announce the intended merger of art and pop. "Marry the Night" (*Born This*

1   Theodor Adorno, *Aesthetic Theory,* trans. Robert Hullot-Kentor (Minneapolis & London: University of Minnesota Press, 1997), 136. Translation altered.

Way) vs. "Aura" (*Artpop*) as opener: a pop tune looking to please everyone (and did!) versus an opening track that risks it all. Here, in "Aura," Gaga announces the tone and intent of the album: to shake things up! Isn't this the essence of both art and pop? Gaga and her producers, engineers, and other talent return to this point of origin across the album as if creating hooks that are also positions in the particular quantum experience she desires for her listeners. Southwest USA experimental soundscapes support absolutely badass backing tracks that drive the song forward to what amounts to a drop/breakdown meets chorus hook. '70s-style disco hooks (Abba-esque) and '80s R&B samples (Chaka Kahn, perhaps) and hits (stutter steps that build toward fully realized phrasing) are blended inside a Launchpad smoothie that gives an analog/digital boost to a tune that may otherwise have been pushed back to later tracks. Instead, this one speaks to the digital and physical presence Gaga becomes across the album and in her Artrave stadium events. The track gives the listener a lot of information to process (rhythms and counter-rhythms, layers upon layers of hooks and samples, returns and bursts). It provokes thinking and dancing, reflection and, for me, sketching our DJ remixes to an ending that left me wanting more. (Which is the whole point of art meshing with pop.) Okay, she seems to say: make something! Remix me. Hack me. That is, even in the first track of *Artpop*, the "announcement," you get the impression that she is very much aware that her work, while presented as a whole, is hardly complete. This is where the listener, the fan, the critic, maybe even the philosopher enters the listening stage: by way of this uncanny clearing of expectations found within the first pronouncement. The outro push is particularly masterful; and a tease.

2

"Venus" is an epic dance tune with Abba, Chic, Donna Summer, and Erasure influences, to say the least. Like "Fashion of His Love," this song brings forward an entire genre of somewhat forgotten electronic post-disco music soundscapes, beats, and hooks into a moment of great EDM uncertainty. The age of the 45; the small studios outside Chicago, New York City, Philly, Berlin, London, and countless other towns and cities: this cosmic soundscape has bold ambitions, like its auteur. As with "Aura," the chorus serves as a break; but the bottom and the playful synthetics are non-stop and carry through the entire tune. Transformational. When Gaga drives "take me to your planet," you realize immediately that she is one of the strongest singer/songwriters in the business today. (Yet for some reason the world needed a *Sound of Music* medley to fully hear her.) The buildup also teases a dubstep "break" possibility, but doesn't go there. Other artists would've taken this as an opportunity to show off their EDM cred (and embarrass themselves trying). The second chorus collects and remixes the backtracking sequences the listener just experienced, introducing the guitar riffs and additional hooks that will define the outro. Gaga's planetary "roll call" marches the listener across the universe to one of the album's best lines: "Don't you know my ass is famous." When a breakdown is announced, she moves to the chorus and drive – backtracks are pushing and then the acoustic guitars hit the counter-melody while the rest of the arrangement drives with 2+4 disco emphasis that is nothing less than perfect. How is this a less mature listening experience, again? Failure?

3

"G.U.Y." strikes me still as an uncanny (familiar yet strange) song whose complexities may be missed on first or second listen. I certainly cannot hear its ingenious architecture on the radio or television. (We discuss in the main discussion some of the problems users and industry producers are experiencing as a function of the imbalance between FM experiences and digital, studio quality playback on iPhones and advanced headphones on the mainstream market. It has the simultaneous feel of an infomercial and Zen koan, a balance between pop and art reminiscent of New Order's unique ability to drive a hook and keep counter melodies alive without the laziness found in most pop tunes. In the bigger picture of *Artpop,* this is the medium tempo jam announced and threaded into the album's fabric across the first two tunes. A slow expanding sound design creates an "unfolding" of the soundscape in a way that fills the epic size of the arrangement. Bridges harken back to "Born this Way" '80s-styled arrangements. I cannot help but think I'm listening to an advanced, enhanced, tricked out Casio keyboard retrofitted into the absolute latest Launchpad hard and software. To perfection. In another refreshingly '80s manner, Gaga and the production team transmit a "too cool for school" affect in both Casio-styled lines and the chorus ("I wanna be your" pick-up lines), which also serves as the basis for one of the most memorable hooks on an album of seemingly endless hooks and motifs. The '80s metal-inspired drive to the end is legion, especially when you consider the way two generations of synthesis and analog are invoked and displayed in a simple eight-bar break.

4

"Sexxx Dreams." Dare I say it: this song is "in" then "out" asking the question: can a bitch play a little game of Pop Diva T&A, FFS? Absolutely. Inspired by Giorgio Moroder (of *Flashdance* soundtrack fame) this track is playful, sexual, and sensual. Yet it also winks in a self-deprecating way at its own peep show spectacle quality, especially with the porny-bass lines during the disco breakdown. Four tracks in and Gaga and her team are still driving the sound design found at the top of the album deeper and farther than any other production team in recent music memory. (Daft Punk's collaborations with Moroder and Nile Rogers deserve mention here.) Then, without announcement, the tune stages an '80s takeover when it links analog-styled sixteenth-note sequencing with the seemingly infinite block-rocking-Launchpads. Gaga schools her competition and critics on how it pulls it all together in the choruses. The arrangement is also a mixed medium where verses have bridge feels and breakdowns emerge from under quarter note drives harkening back to En Vogue and Destiny's Child, occasionally Beyonce – always Janet Jackson and Mary J. Blige.

5

"Jewels N' Drugs" harkens back to the crazy syncopated, low budget "mixtape" world of 50 Cent. This deceptively simple tune has a driving, hump-thump-bump-n-grind comprised of some of the most used Millennial hip-hop riffs. Yet, given the artpop context of the tune, I cannot help but hear an underlying critique of hip-hop too, especially when she blurs the lines between social critique of materialism, the need for pop culture to lighten the fuck up ("try to have some fuckin fun") in middle breakdown and the intensification of hip-hop hyper-sexuality ("good pussy in the passenger seat"). This track also undermines its own sense of authority as hip-hop or art or pop or underground mixtape because the sheer amount of hooks make it a deconstruction of the entire genre. I especially love how the outro serves as a breakdown recorded with the intent to school the industry, not to entertain her fans. While I personally would've loved to hear some dub drops and a wider, deeper sound architecture, I can hear (and see, check out SXSW performance of this tune) why she leaves herself the room to ride it out rather than bass drop into a new section. (Some serious Long Island, New Jersey, Manhattan back-window bass in this track provokes laughter and neck bobbing like it's 1989.) As with "Sexxx Dreams," this one sounds like it could be an end credit commercial ditty, with the "Jewels N' Drugs" hook that accompanies you as you walk from the movie auditorium to the long Cineplex corridors to the exit a few feet from the last standing *Pac Man* console in a thousand miles.

6

"MANiCURE" is where the album pivots again by re-introducing the pop master style and all that accompanies it: hooks, rides, drives, lifts, etc. Unlike "Jewels N' Drugs," this song is a straight pop tune. Yet, it has an anthemic and playful 1950s bubble gum backbeat in a way popularized by Taylor Swift and Pharrell Williams. I also cannot help but think this is Gaga throwing the gauntlet down to Katy Perry. (Which is fun, not controversial.) The signature Gaga breakdown is one of the best on the album, this time featuring guitar and big beat drums. This song displays a similar chorus structure to earlier tracks, yet "MANiCURE" is not repetitive in the least; the subtle differences keep the listener on board a very different pop train than *Born This Way*. Finally, the halftime outro picks up where "Jewels N' Drugs" left off, implying that "MANiCURE" may be an extension of the previous track. I'd personally like to see this track get a wide release (which may be difficult as it's been in the pipe since December 2013).

7

"Do What You Want" reveals that *Artpop* is a total experience as each track, especially this one, repeatedly reaches back to the soundtrack breakouts of the '70s (*Saturday Night Fever*) and '80s (*Flashdance* and *Footloose*) to give the middle tracks the narrative quality of a fictitious unreleased blockbuster. As one of the strongest R&B tracks of 2013, this self-confident synth celebration features breakdown moments expected of a track featuring R. Kelly (not to mention the Cristina Aguilera duet on *The Voice*, December 2013). Once again, an Erasure-inspired backtrack and design also somehow invokes the spirit of Donna Summer (especially "Love to Love You Baby"). By this point in the album, a progression of themes and styles coalesce to announce (preview, prefigure, predict) some form of a pop music takedown. In other words, what I hear in *Artpop* by the time we get to "Do What You Want" is an artist speaking directly to her Little Monsters, past the pop critics, the many haters, the fanboys – all of them at once – offering a very simple whisper somewhere between the tracks, main plot lines – I cannot help but sense her smiling with the foreknowledge that "Gypsy" and "Applause" are coming. But, like a good artist, she's also cautioning us, "but, not yet." I also hear her saying "school's in session."

8

"Artpop" is the Everlasting Gobstopper of ear candy. Gaga brings together three generations of sound with Lipps, Inc., Abba, Jamiroquai-inspired architecture that also harkens back to the '90s electronica of Chemical Brothers, Crystal Method, Blur, and Gorillaz. This tune deserves its title track status; it's an anthemic pronouncement harkening back to '70s disco and '80s epic pop. This kind of tune must make Cher smile especially the drive/lift in the center of the arrangement where a sonorous seismic event transpires in the headphones and PA digital surround sound system. Add to this art/pop mixture an adrenaline-draining, hypnotic string arrangement and what you get is an experimental sounding song that reaches out to as many audiences as possible. Lady Gaga's performance of this song on *The Tonight Show* premiere week displays the song's ability (not to mention the profound television direction it inspired) to reach out through mass media directly into the multiverse of her audience's particular positions. She is one and many with one and many different people... an example of the multiplicity she experiences as an artist (see "Mary Jane Holland" below) as well as the multi-faceted object of iconic desire (same for "Applause"). It is also worth noting that her performance on Jimmy Fallon's *Tonight Show* (Feb. 18, 2014) is one of the best segments on live television, standing next to Future Islands on *David Letterman* (March 3, 2014), Miley Cyrus (October 5, 2013), and Prince (November 1, 2014) on *Saturday Night Live,* and Mute Math on *Jimmy Kimmel* (September 19, 2007)

9

"Swine" is late-'80s techno kicking around with emerging '90s trance in a 2010s EDM/House time warp that sets off an audio explosion made by a lethal cocktail of size, drive, and edge best found across the *Born This Way* album (especially "Judas"). It is impossible not to feel absolutely schooled by the innovative Launchpad break downs and the guttural, open synth analog goodness manifesting the arpeggiated, beautifully filtered sound architecture found earlier in "Aura" and "G.U.Y.". This tune represents, for me, one of the best house moments of 2013: a '70s bridge/lift after the instrumental breakdown. Again, Giorgio Moroder's synthesis in "Flashdance." The backing tracks and lower frequency sequences work the neurons over like a Zomboy and Zedd track especially as "Swine" expands on its original hooks and concepts to absolutely dominate the album's intended art/pop merger through the drops that fragment and fracture into quarter note drives and touchpad breaks and break beats unlike anything ("g-g-grab the beat") Gaga has recorded since "Love Game." "Swine" was performed at SXSW (March 2014) to much controversy given the presence of vomit artist Millie Brown. Even though Gaga introduced "Swine" as a rape protest song, most major media outlets focused on bulimia because, I guess, Demi Lovato said so.

10

"Donatella" announces a glam/pop culture trilogy that is pulled right from the stadium icons Gaga calls her heroes: Bowie, Freddie, Mick, Stevie Nicks. This tune performs an uncanny dance meditation on fashion and fame, neither a critique nor an embrace of the very industry that helped to create Lady Gaga the megastar. Is it possible to be in the middle of an event like a celebrity fashion show and also be positioned as the observer of such an event? Sure: if you think and live in many dimensions you can; and these three tracks move Lady Gaga – the character, the person, the celebrity, the daughter, the boss, the fashion icon, the vulnerable friend – across the multiverse of her aural expressions into a short story trilogy that starts with "Donatella." Both, the lyrics and score to this narrative almost sound as though intended to show how this character called Gaga is lost in the mix, all the chaos, all the movement, the complexity of a life lived live, as the site of multiple meaning. After all, hundreds of millions of people project onto her their own desire, need, hope, horror, joy, faith, despair; I am but one of these masses writing and talking back to the woman who finds herself commanded to "run down the runway but don't puke." Gaga's team shows great restraint in the breakdown during the last movement of the song... pushes to drive but breaks away. Gentle acoustic orchestration including a gentle ride cymbal fades in. Then, an epic disco build. Back to runway trance/electronica. No lyrics. Instrumental drive. A moment where this character is celebrated; a brief moment. Then a final breakdown. And an abrupt end.

11

"Fashion!" is a tune that offers a glimpse into the deeper narrations of a woman who exists in many different places at one time (à la David Bowie): the singer, the fashion icon, the tabloid personae, the performer. It's as though through the role of "Donatella," Gaga is able to cross through some kind of time/space, bounce back and forth saying: "I own the world / we own the world." She is both diva and divination. Looking good and feeling fine, a slightly menacing presence in the breakdowns. The guttural bass lines imply a seriousness for this crazy blend of critique, whimsy, epic cultural event called the runway of Gaga's mind. This all unravels in "Mary Jane Holland." The tune is almost a "No Exit" (manic existential remix) of fashion – Hell or Heaven? Where are we? Who is Lady Gaga? Yet, while these questions are explored and asked in the music and the subtext of the chorus lyrics, Gaga's definitely comfortable with performing as the uber-diva on this one, unlike in "Donatella" where the transformation across identities is a bit unsure. Here, on the other hand, you get lyrics like: "I feel on top of the world" and "looking good and feeling fine." Still a bit detached with echoes of Donatella in one range/frequency of the sound design. There's also a story happening that you will miss the first time listening to these middle tracks: Lady Gaga's uber-diva seems to have captured Donatella. By the breakdown, the song devolves. Donatella has been lured in and captured by "Fashion the fashion."

12

"Mary Jane Holland" stages a Faustian wager where the heroin(e) is tempted along the way by the Fame Monster. She resists the last two options for this figure: "Make deals with every devil inside." This one strikes me as a recovery tune, an attempt to recover (anticipating "Dope"), where the heroin(e) becomes something more than just "fashion." Perhaps this strange, groovy, fun tune is a bit of an escape to "Mary Jane" and "Holland" (pot capital of the world), replete with a glam rock bridge from the days of The Who's *Tommy*: the MC introduction especially. (Her '70s inspirations are found all across the second half of this song.) For such a personal song, this arrangement is gigantic, epic in the Bertolt Brecht sense of the word. Familiar and strange; seeing Lady Gaga differently with each movement. This may be my favorite track on the album (behind "Gypsy," as you'll shortly read). When "Mary Jane Holland" reaches its conclusion, Gaga becomes (yet again) someone else, a fully realized Mary Jane Holland, thus concluding the "fashion/pop" trilogy with a lingering sense of angst and desperation. In other words, where's Stefani Germanotta? For that matter, where's Lady Gaga? "She" (all of her) is lost inside the "Aura" of the opening track, which is not necessarily a good thing. The song melts away, something is wrong – perhaps Alice has travelled too far down the Rabbit Hole.

13

"Dope" is the penultimate destination for the entire *Artpop* album: rock bottom... acoustic... a song of atonement... literally "a" state of "tonement" in the design... the sequenced background... the sound design of Vince Clarke and Andy Bell (Erasure). Echoes of the Depeche Mode *Violator* album that defined Generation X electronica.

But the moment belongs to Freddie Mercury and Queen who must all smile knowing that the woman who was inspired by "Radio Ga Ga" is here in this track not just paying homage to her own acoustic and compositional roots but also opening up the possibilities for the final two songs, "Gypsy" and "Applause." Gaga seems to say that without the journey, why bother? This song carries the listener close to the perfection she's been striving for as an artist across the entire album; this time, great art did not disappoint.

This is all to reveal…

All of it – the entire album…

Now you get the best pop song written since The Beatles' "Hey Jude" and Michael Jackson's "We Are the World"…

Old school…

14

"Gypsy" is the answer to the epic question haunting my listening experience across *Artpop*: where is all of this going? Simple. This album is a gathering, a calling forth of the users into the heart of Gaga's aural kingdom – bringing everyone together in this track. The gypsy has arrived home. When I first heard the song while carrying on the first of many interviews across Fall 2013 and 2014, I said: thank God, she's home. This is where she needs to be, allowing herself to "be alone together" with herself and all the hundreds of millions who love her. Her secret weapon against her detractors or saboteurs is joy, love, and scary pure unmistakable and unapologetic talent. Pure and simple. Here I am, she says. I am *all* of these people, all of these stories. All at once. Also, this is the single to end all singles, the one that would have been on the charts for months like back in the '80s. Like Michael. So this song is more than just an '80s anthem, it's an intergenerational hack into the coded being of the Top 40 construct. Sorry, haters: this song is perfect. It is the accumulation of track after track of self-exploration and multiple presentations of both art and pop. The road metaphors and the upbeat tone of the song could be something you'd find in a *Godspell* or *Wiz* revival! Gaga's writing embraces the anthemic reach of Journey ("Faithfully," "Only the Young," and "Be Good to Yourself"). The gigantic hooks and joyful drives share studio space with Billy Joel ("Piano Man," "Scenes from an Italian Restaurant," and "I Go to Extremes") while also revealing her inner Elton John ("Saturday Night Is Alright for Fighting," "Rocketman," and "I'm Still Standing"). Perhaps this track is her "Radio Gaga" (Queen) yet seems to diverge into frontiers forged by Carole King, Carly Simon, and Cher. Like the ending of Grease, she pulls it all together, then blasts off again!

15

"Applause" displays a "roll credits" and almost hypnotic quality. Interestingly, it was the first major release in the States. This tune also has the power to overtake (revise/deconstruct) the previous fourteen-track listening experience. Halfway through this final track, I started to question whether I had indeed heard what I heard across the whole album. This is a very unnerving experience, a quantum event and experience that caused me to think again about the album, the thoughts generated by the tracks, and the overall experience of something that is so much more than a pop release. This track redefines the relationship between the listener and Gaga, perhaps best described as an I/thou moment. Something surface and deep. Up-tempo fun. Deceptive. Like she's just having a good time and yet, in the midsts of this headphones party, while she has our attention, she offers a universal lesson all artists, even philosophers, need to learn: it is impossible to please everyone. She, like me, at the end of the day, will be perceived as a "coont." But it is all worth it, she also seems to say. Without the excesses, without overstaying our welcome, the album, like this book, would've failed. Thank you, and fuck you.

ACKNOWLEDG-
MENTS

"'Be grateful to everyone' is about making peace with the aspects of ourselves that we have rejected... If we were to make a list of people we don't like – people we find obnoxious, threatening, or worthy of contempt – we would discover much about those aspects of ourselves that we can't face... other people trigger the karma that we haven't worked out."

– Pema Chödrön

The conclusion of my first book, *Itself*, is a seventeen-page sentence. A long meditation of sorts attempting to locate and house, for a moment, the thoughts that were escaping me in the last days of the revision process for both the dissertation and manuscript. I won't subject my readers to that particular kind of endurance test again. So, the final thoughts that follow are mostly focused on thanking everyone who supported this work, especially when its fate seemed most uncertain across 2015.

I've lived in an analog and digital world my entire life. Inside my headphones – from the days of the blessed 45″ to MySpace to iTunes to Pandora on a MacBook, I've encountered a vast universe of memories, images, fragments, directives, reflections, interdimensional thinking located between the ears. A rave populated by the dead and the living, the forgotten and the remembered, the invited and the uninvited. I can say without any hesitation that my time with Stefani marks one of the few times I've been able to share fully this auratic life. "Holy fuck, Shelly. She 'gets' it... She completely 'gets' it..." (February 2014).

Moments when I would retreat into the headphones included mourning the death of my father (Talking Heads' "Stop Making Sense"), resisting the endless fascism of the public school system (my yellow Sony Sports Walkman), attempting to filter in the new thoughts and ways of looking at the world I encountered in Washington, DC, at Catholic University (1988–92), surrounding myself with a USS Enterprise sound shield when my best friend's father committed suicide in 1991, time and space traveling with my then-girlfriend now-wife, Michelle, across New England in the early to mid-'90s – all those mixed tapes and new CDs and hundreds of miles of driving. What a gift!

Then there's Montauk, NY – the end of the Island. September 1987. The release of Rush and Pink Floyd that month, the albums haters and poseur fans described as "sellouts" achieved eternal status in my circle of friends. Across a long party weekend, we played Rush's *Hold Your Fire* and Pink Floyd's *A Momentary Lapse of*

Reason with such repetition that I could hear the keyboards and symphonic tracks even when sleeping. Turtle Cove was the destination. The east end ocean was also where I first "tranceived" information, ideas, feelings, ways of experiencing the world that were markedly quite different from how my friends were engaging and disengaging the world we were thrown into that year.

September 1987 to August 1988 were transitional in very traditional ways. High school to college for me; high school to jobs for others; and still others high school to the total chaos of a world that doesn't give a fuck about them. Get a job. Do something. Go to community college. Deal drugs. Drive for Dominoes. Work at a liquor store. Telemarketing seemed like a good option for a lot of people.

I know I jumped a quantum plane that weekend.

I know I've been jumping quite a few across the twenty-nine years since.

I know very little but what I do know amounts to this: "One slip and down the hole you fall / it seems to take, no time at all" (Pink Floyd, "One Slip").

My point is simple: music saves and creates and sustains lives. It is filled with surprises and reassurances, sometimes the unknowns can sound and feel terrifying. But that uncertainty, that anxiety, is part of life. At least in the headphones, I always had company.

It's not an accident Stefani and I found each other in the midst of the chaos of our personal and professional lives. I am extremely grateful for her intercession, as well as for the many months of companionship I enjoyed. Before, during, and after those conversations, many people helped to keep me sane, employed, and believing in this project when during some very dark times – the closing of Lebanon College across the Fall of 2014 – it seemed all was lost, this project was dead.

Here's a short description and list of the rock stars who jammed with me over the last years while I created this project:

Stefani Germanotta was nothing less than the Mother Monster and Eternal Mistress that others have discussed and described in public. Up until Fall 2013, I had never met someone other than my wife Michelle with such quick wit. Gaga struggles with immediate and sustained insights into herself and the many different industries she dominates. Her generosity to me and my family, her ongoing support of this project, and her impeccable and unstoppable talents as a *philosopher* remain unmatched. I hope our conversation will influence generations to come. I also hope this project silences the "bleaters of connivance" (Adorno) who like to tell Stefani and me and others like us what the fuck to do when they need to step back and thank whatever God they're not following we are all working together toward a common goal of excellence and inspirational mediated moments in this life world (Schirmacher).

For the Facebook group support while communicating with Stefani, special thanks to Crestin Davis, George Elerick, Dawn Shank Glatfelter, J. Jack Halberstam, Katerina Kolozova, Claudia Landolfi, Manuel Vargas Rcld, Tony Yanik, and Sean Witty.

Pema Chödrön's *Uncomfortable with Uncertainty* is still the most important book I consulted these past five or so years attempting to launch all entertainment and education projects. I also found great solace in *Mysticism* by Evelyn Underhill. Most entrepreneur books are shite with the exception of my dear mentor Ryan Blair's *Nothing to Lose, Everything to Gain.*

Gibson DelGuidici, Giovanni Gambino, Geoffrey Garfield, Kevin Glover, Richard Haase, Maria Nieto, John Solomon, Michael Waterman, and many others from my New York City and Los Angeles producing team have fought alongside me on countless media projects since 2011. I cannot thank them enough for their years of hand-to-hand project combat. This one, however, was my first solo work, an attempt to bring together (again) the academic and the entertainment sides of a career that began and ended in New England, from Dartmouth College (1995) to Lebanon College (2014).

Harry Lennix may never fully understand the deep gratitude I hold very close to my heart in light of his most generous participation in the Adam Clayton Powell Jr. project, whose own development and stage history parallels the strange, difficult, and unorthodox writing and editorial process that helped me complete *Thoughtrave.*

Frank Perricone and the Bear Jam Studios family in Long Beach, CA, helped set this off in September 2012 with a week's long retreat that immediately helped me understand the core mission of my work – to bring three generations together in media projects that will completely surprise the industries that control the current conversation about music, television, film, theater, and education. Thank you also for the hair care tips.

None of this work would have mattered if it weren't for my students over the years at Dartmouth College, University of Minnesota–Twin Cities, the Community College of Vermont, River Valley Community College, Southern New Hampshire University, Franklin Pierce University, Lebanon College, and the European Graduate School. Across Fall 2015, my students at Fordham University Lincoln Center and St. John's University encouraged me to finish this book when I was most doubtful it would ever see the light of day beyond the Pirate Bay hack (September 2015) or a series of pdf exchanges with media studies and music colleagues (March 2014–November 2015).

At Fordham Lincoln Center: John Badagliacca, Paige Bryan, Megan Coyle-Howard, Tina Dantono, Aurpita Deb, Jack DeWahl, Eamon Duke, Keira Edgett, Audrey Fenter, Matthew Gallipoli, Ilyssa Guerra, Karin Hadadan, Lara Heard, Kara Hogan, Catherine Korsh, Olivia Labarge, Colette Lanzon, Angela Lavarello, Anastasia Mahoney, Annamarie Nistico, Genevieve O'Brien, Amanda Peralta, Maria Julia Pieraccioni, Ellie Sato, Jaclyn Scerbak, Colin Sheeley, Brenna Slane, Abigail Velasquez, Aidan Wheeler, Kayce Wilson, and Eamon Wolfgram.

At St. John's University: Dotun Akinsade, Antonio Alvarez, Kimberly Brown, Kaylin Cruz, Angela Gallo, Angela Lavarello, Remington McCutcheon, Amanda Medina, Marcello Menucci, Terynn Mingo, Elijah Ortiz, William Pabitero, Avana Ramkistodas, Devonte Reid-Thompson, Karla Saltos, Ryan Schneider, Nathan Silva, Raeven Small, Lorena Teixeira, Yerlin Urena-Suero, Scott Waltke, Sadiera Washington.

For my adjunct (at-will, contingent) friends who never once stopped fighting alongside me, especially when I ran away from Adjunctland, picking me up when the Badmin(istrators) and their media lackeys and attorneys would attempt to mow us over with publicity or new policies. The fight for teachers and students in higher education brought together a diverse, national, and interdimensional (second life) group of people who changed my life: Lee Skallerup Bessette, Brianne Bolin, Anne Clune, George Elerick, Joe Fruscione, Mary Grace Gainer, Genevieve Jacobs, Kat Jacobsen, Seth Kahn, Rick Kissell, Lee Kottner, Alex Kudera, David Long, Maria Maisto Lynch, T.L. MackPico, Karen Lentz Madison, Dana Biscotti Myskowski, Rebecca Schuman, Siobhan Senier,

Dahn Shaulis, Murray J. Siskind, Lydia Field Snow, Maria Shine Stewart, Desirée Sunshine, and David B. Wilder.

Lamia Vardic Kosovic jumped into my projects and life with intensity, intelligence, and fidelity during the darkest moments of 2015 when we were literally shipwrecked as a family, between residences and without work. What some call "destitute," but I hesitate using that word for the sole reason that we had family and friends to help us out in every way needed. Lamia and I are working together to create Wisdom1096, a "scale free" education platform that also serves to restart the academic clock by way of an Oxford styled tutorial emphasis and grounding in the affinity that binds everyone in my current personal, spiritual, and professional life: staging a brutal, sustained attack on higher education the way Stefani has described a liberational program launched within the music industry against the music industry.

Catherine Kleinhans is nothing less than a miracle: a friend, a publicist, a collaborator, a conspirator, a midnight YouTube rabbit hole traveler. There is no way the Haus of Baum would have made it this far without your faith, hope, love, and obsessions with Robert Redford's *Electric Horsemen* and all things '80s music, new wave, and ridiculous gatherings of internet memes, clips, and whole channels. Thank you, dear one.

For the wisdom, leadership, support, and unflinching day-to-day operational help during the closing of Lebanon College (August 2014), I want to thank no one on the Board of Trustees or Advisers. Instead, I want to acknowledge the students, staff, faculty, and administrative team who helped me transition a twenty-year academic career into writing, producing, composing, and publicity life I have enjoyed, with all the ups and downs of starting a new professional life. My colleague of ten years, Ron Biron, never once stopped encouraging me to finish this book as well as explore ways to do more high profile media work, even from my stranded location on Green Street in Lebanon, NH.

My Facebook family (which also crosses over into my high school, college, and graduate school life) has been in my second digital life since about 2008. I can't list everyone, but I really want to take a moment to acknowledge people who sat with me over the years. There is nothing worse to experience alone as a writer and producer than the endless uncertainty and silence of those in-between moments of a negotiation or project redraft and so forth:

Stephanie Adams, The Alexander Family, Paul and Ann Allen, Tania Arens, Mike Argenziano, Trillian Astra, Betty Raines Azwell, Anthony Barca, Kelissa Java Bhnidi, Andres Borderias, Danielle Brewer, Clinton Canaday, Cheryl Carrabba, Carol ChiChester, Ellyn Conway Robbins Cole, Anthony Collins, Vincent Commisso, Greg Dash, Warm Heatherette Davis, Mike De Allende, Shawn Decker, Travis Dennison, Bill DesJardins, April Doherty, David Domena, Timothy Duggan, Laura Gatewood Eldridge, Emily Elizabeth, Stephen Fishman, Nancy Baker Fowler, Stanley Gemmeli, Rebecca Gibson, Zillah Glory, Dean Goddard, Beverly Goodman, Suzanne Gordon, Frank Gorman, Richard Greenman, John Gryn, Linda Hammersten, Guy L.W. Hardy, Lauren Hardy, Kate Shogi Hinds, Stacy L. Strader Hogsett, Joe Hurley, Mariya Morse Hurwitz, Chris Jett, Joseph Johnson, Bobby Jones, Anne-Marie Reuter Kane, Kitara Kara, Stacey Keith, Doris Kennedy, Peter Kennett, David Kidd, Ryan King, Amy Knight, Michael Paul Kròl, Dan Kupka, Amanda Lesnick, Jimmy Liss, J. Holt Littlefield, Siddhartha Lokanandi, Nancy Kilmer, Earl Knudsen (d. 1991), Erik Knudsen, Karl Knudsen, Ruth Knudsen, Ron Liddel, Amanda Lagor McElhaney, Holly McIntosh, Charlotte Donna McIntyre, Michèle Mercier, Rizzo Mertz, Pat Murray, Matt Naj, Eric Nelson, Robert Nichols, Nicola Nicola, Molly O'Hara, Christopher Parker, Sheri Ponzi, Moe Profane, Alicia Rawson, Zachary Reinhardt, William Edward Rieffer, Sam Robbins, Seth Rogin, Alison (and Brian and Stella) Rose, Jim Æloi Rose, Isaac Rounseville, Jeremy Ruzanski, Leigh Salvage, Elizabeth Schmitt, Patricia Logue Smith, Zachary Sneddon, Steven Strawmatt, James Swift, Piret Vaher, Helga Weiss, Rachel Chas Williams, Alex Young, and Allison McMaster Young.

For Karen Kirsti Adger: thank you for all your help publicizing and managing the *Thoughtrave* digital universe.

Leo Andoh Korash and McLaren Sforza never lost faith in me, let alone my projects. Through their intercession, Leo and McLaren served "last watch of the night" duty with me and my family as we found ourselves unable to remain part of the Universal Church (2009–2015).

I can't thank my son George's online friends enough for keeping him company and helping him develop his writing and performing voice: Sylvia Harris, Sylvester Pendergast, Proto Rvd, Tommy Williams, and the Arielrocks9 crew at www.letterboxd.com.

George, Jess, Eli, Caden, Colby, and Tate Roe for coming along for the ride–don't worry, you didn't have a choice.

Jason Cilio was the Eagle who flew up from Rhode Island to help me with a production that would have completely died if he didn't arrive just in time with food, drink, and an "all hands on deck" attitude. This concert restored my will and faith to complete *Thoughtrave.*

Jonathan Blum probably doesn't know it, but his brutally honest critiques of earlier education platforms resulted in the present versions of both entertainment and education projects. I asked him for one thing and one thing only: be objective. The game shifted for me around 2010–11. He was a very important voice in the exploratory and prototype phase of everything that's transpired in the last five or so years.

John Pontrelli basically told me to walk the fuck away or fight within every inch of my life for the shows, music, films, and platforms that I hope will define that crazy thing called "a legacy." I think the bags under my eyes will tell you how I responded to his warning.

Joe Landolfi and I have lived very different lives but we always come back to a source, a place where ideas and rhythms and a lifelong friendship was formed in his mother's basement on Richardson Lane in Islip: a drum set and a few keyboards. Special thanks to Flo, Hunter, and Hannah for their hospitality during the most difficult of times in August/September 2015.

Jennifer Jeran will always be the cool one; everything I do is a feeble attempt to keep up with her badass attitude and outlook. Thank you for taking good care of Bobby Baum for so long.

Special thanks for the love and food and drink and insider's glimpse of Los Angeles goes to Steven Guilmette, Christine Bianculli Guilmette, Michael Starr, and the fugitives from easily the most aggressive and soul-damning game of "Cards Against Humanity" (July 2015).

At the Main Street Museum, I found my Island of Misfit toys. A place of healing, audacity, and love. Eternal thanks to Eric Cram, Laura Di Piazza, Tim Duggan, Chico Esteridge, David Fairbanks Ford, Bunny Harvey, Mark Merrill, Barbara Stevens, Robert Stone, and Mark Waskow. Special shout out to Donna and Chris (Donna Thunders band), James McSheffrey, Venlo, and the What Doth Life family.

Peter Money and Bill Craig and I moved through and beyond Upper Valley New Hampshire and Vermont arts and education circles for more than two decades. At every transition point, I would find Peter and Bill. Thank you both for haunting all that I do.

Luke Chrisinger is the most important and life-changing artist of his generation. He planned *Thoughtrave* events with me and offered his catalog to the world, thousands of songs and other files. Other than the late Aaron Swartz, I can't think of a more vocal and important advocate of open media culture and corporate-free music.

Former students and current minions of doom: Thomas R. Bishop, Brianne Bolin, Kevin Chartier, Ryan Chartier, Margaret Eckert, Jeff Guthrie, Cherilyn Hautanen, Mike Heenan, Philip Horner-Richardson, Nathan Keyes, Ace Adam Lodestone, Dana McNeil, Rachel Michele Potter, Karen Sager, Bianca Tom, Steve Woods, and Liza Wyman.

Billie Jo Konze and Kyle Matthew Roberts worked with me in the earliest days of these projects, in the corner of an Irish café that is now a pierogy factory in Quechee, VT. "They Fade, the Words Fade" was a revival of Dennis Moritz's theater as a long-distance shout-out to the Lower East Side that resulted in an eventual performance at the old Bowery Poetry Club featuring In Example (What Doth Life artists) and G. Ellroy McMullen/Skronklife (Greg McMullen). I mention these people and this event because they reminded me of a "me" I had lost touch with over the academic and poverty-line years.

Nancy Marashio (2003–11) resurrected and nourished with the tough love of Ra's al Ghul (*Batman Begins*) and Pai Mei (*Kill Bill Vol. 2*) to help create this RCB character. Without her support in 2011 and 2012, I am quite convinced *Thoughtrave* and other projects would never have seen the light of day let alone high noon.

Marlene Lewis was more than a staff member at River Valley Community College. She became one of my strongest advocates for the student-centered and fearless mission I tried to reinforce in every course I taught or workshop I led or platform I designed. After RVCC, she always checked in with me. I recruited her for Lebanon College. She was there for me and my family when the Board threw in the towel. I think the best word to describe her friendship and love and collegiality is "sentinel."

Spencer Lewis produced tracks for me as well as jammed on some new thoughts and techniques I brought with me to Gilead, his home and studio in Bethel, VT. Just hitting the record button and hanging out with someone whose music has been in my headphones and sound systems since 1993 was a thrill. Finding a friend and brutally honest collaborator was more than I deserved. Thank you, Spencer of "Approaching Love" and "Opening," especially (available on the Robert Craig Baum Soundcloud page).

Doug Anderson has been a friend since Minneapolis–St. Paul days 1998–2001. With him back in Brooklyn and this book behind me, I am looking forward to getting into trouble in the Lower East Side and wherever bad choices take us. (While writing this section, Doug wrote: "Let's start a fucking band." And indeed we did.)

Cornel West returned to my life in February 2016 exactly when I started to rethink and regroup how best to move forward my academic and entertainment work simultaneously. He was one of a few people to really sit with me and mourn the loss of Lebanon College as well as my academic career. We met while I was working for and collaborating with August Wilson at Dartmouth 1997–98. We spent a weekend before that with Edward Said (d. 2003) in 1996 where "After Orientalism" was convened at Columbia University's Italian Academy. He was also a wonderful collaborator with my students at the Community College of Vermont. "You' on fire, Brother Baum" was all I needed to hear to know 2016 would be a year of great reconciliation and renewal.

Harold Bloom sat with me Fall 2014 after the doors closed. On a dark and stormy morning at the top of November 2014, I drove down from Lebanon, NH, to sit at the feet of my master. We discussed the future of higher education, the role the "School of Resentment" played in the neoliberal takeover of the budgets and tenure lines, the downsizing of everything. Mostly, he was a kind mentor who took time to enjoy a cup of tea with one of his biggest fans and most respectful and unyielding adversaries. He encouraged and delighted in *Thoughtrave*.

Colleagues old and new: Giorgio Agamben, Udi Aloni, Senka Anastasova, Michael Anker, Sinan Antoon, Selcuk Artut, Alain Badiou, Geoffrey Bell, Jeffrey Bernstein, Jennifer Blackmer, Sharon Bridgforth, Melissa Bruninga, Dorothy Bukay, Drew Burk, Laurie Carlos, Hannes Charen, Walter Dallas, Christopher Danowski,

Clinton Turner Davis, Vladmir Dritsas, Atom Egoyan, Jeremy Fernando, Mike Figgis, Christopher Fynsk, Matthew Tyler Giobbi, Henry Giroux, Matthias Goertz, Anthony Gow, Peter Greenaway, D. Kat Griggs, Adam Staley Groves, Werner Hamacher, Moraig Henderson, Matthew Keenan, Michal Kobialka, Sonja Kuftinec, Rob Larson, Sarah Larson, Andreas Levi, Henry MacWilliams, Marina Masic, Jaques-Alain Miller, Matthew Mitchem, Dennis Moritz, Moh Mouhoubi, Jean-Luc Nancy, Derek Owens, Greg Palast, Donald E. Pease, Jason Read, Michael Rectenwald, Julie Reshe, Duane Rousselle, Edward Said (d. 2003), Wolfgang Schirmacher, Wuhan Slim, Kent Stevens, Sandy Stone, Mike Teg, Alan Trevithick, Tamara Underiner, Jane Van Slembrouck, Victor L. Walker II, April Warn-Vannini, H.E. Whitney, August Wilson (d. 2005), Aleksandra Wolska, and Slavoj Žižek.

Matthew Steven Carlos has been my closest collaborator on philosophical and higher education projects since 2002. I am forever grateful for his unyielding support for all I do as well as willingness to spend four days in Baumtown (Halloween weekend 2015) while we plotted out the next twenty years at my dining room table with my son's white board. To walk along Bryant Park with him after having spent an evening with my sons at the same spot a couple months earlier while on the edge of destitution (far from the "Edge of Glory," so we thought). In the distance at all times, in August and October 2015, was the Grace Building. (Yes, I love symbolism.)

Avital Ronell is a mentor, friend, and inspiration in all manner of things. From New York City to Saas-Fee, Switzerland, back to New York City, Avital embodies all that is right in higher education and all that matters to me especially when it comes to how philosophy changes lives and inspires an utterly fearless engagement with the world in a way that produces the kind of affinity relationships found across this book, especially in the friendship that formed immediately with Stefani and her staff.

Julia Hölzl was another "last watch of the night" comrade who bounced ideas, developed thoughts, explored projects, and laughed at my stupid jokes across some of the darkest days of the last eighteen months especially. (*I eat goats!*)

Adam Lodestone and Bri Bolin are my newest apprentices: faithful, fearless, strong, and unyielding in our mission to restore some kind of sanity (yeah, right, us?) to academics and entertainment.

Adam's TRANSit platforms (transgendered studies and independent media) and Bri's life work as a disabilities advocate, screen/teleplay writer, and exceptional poet (how great are her "Interludes" here in *Thoughtrave*?) are not only vital to the furthering of free, innovative, and community-focused revolutionary thinking, their presence in my life quite honestly saved me from being consumed by confusion, fatigue, rage, and hopelessness. Headphones on, dear ones. You are next!

Danielle Pittel met with Laurie Carlos in the summer of 2014 about a key performance piece that will see the light of day shortly. I was quite sure it was D.O.A. at the time of their gathering. But while meeting and driving around Lake Minnetonka, apparently Dani and Laurie brought it all back to life. At that time, there was very little forward movement on any project, come to think of it. Just a lot of false starts and crash-and-burn. From our first meeting in 1999 at UMN–Twin Cities to now, I have never read or heard Dani express anything but unflinching support for my work (teaching or otherwise) and showing a love for my family that transcends the distance between Minnesota and New York. She believed when I had no more faith to give; she loved when I was filled with rage; she listened when I was unable to even form the words. She is a very good friend to me, and with this project and other pieces moving forward, I hope our clan can finally meet and get to know her daughter, Lilly.

Karen, Warren, Ethan, and the Tom Family went "all-in" with us in 2015–16. I am quite sure this moment of *Thoughtrave* and other project negotiations (new and renewed) would not have been possible without their love and support.

Eileen Joy and Vincent W.J. van Gerven Oei deserve to share MVP status for immediately understanding this project in its political, spiritual, mediated, and philosophical intensity and reach. After having been laughed at by ten separate publishers – because I wanted to retain my rights and strike a partnership regarding all back end film, television, audiobook, etc. – and getting "the high hat" (Barton Fink reference), this writer decided to step back and regroup again. Sometimes it is necessary to stop moving, to position, and to take in all of your surroundings. This essential lesson of Stefani Germanotta and our mutual friend Jason Brooker allowed me and my family to become invisible in public, inaudible while kicking and screaming across 2015, and unyielding in our determination to keep this journey going until we reached some kind of promised land. Strangely, that place turned out to be Long Island again, my home 1970–1993.

Havah, Ryan, Finn, and Mirren Armstrong Walther are part of our extended family, badasses in their own right. Their hard work and uncanny ability to know the exact right time to show up with food and treats or offer to host my kids or encourage us to get out of the house especially when most busy – what a blessing to call them all friends.

Jennifer T'oots (Casey) Trinkle was at the table when this crazy journey started in Fall 1991, a time that is very cloudy and hazy when I think about Washington, DC, and our Shakespeare and Philosophy classes. She keeps telling me she doesn't know who would benefit from her "Writing to Survive" blog. She denies having enough of an audience to publish widely. She has no idea who would even buy such a book of short episodic, occasional, and experimental pieces. Let me cut to the chase: I benefited. I and a few hundred people are her audience. I would buy her book, promote it to the ends of the Earth and beyond. Does that answer your question, Jen?

Justin Norton is another rock star from my CatholicU days, a metal writer now, former "legit" journalist. He is one of my inspirations, someone I've greatly admired for more than two decades now. His writing is infinitely better than mine; his imagination is also a terrifying place to visit. If we weren't living on different coasts, I am quite sure we would need to write our wife's phone numbers in Sharpie on our forearms. And, knowing them, they'd definitely let us rot in the drunk tank until we begged forgiveness and gave false promises to never do *that* again.

Linda and Joe Shaw are absolutely the best in-laws anyone could ask for. Thank you. While struggling through almost two years of great professional, financial, personal, and spiritual uncertainty, these two, along with my extended family in Vermont, New Hampshire, and Massachusetts were vigilant in their unyielding support for the Baums.

For my mother, Margaret Ann Baum for laying the foundation of deep trust in my abilities and talents as well as for programming resilience as a prime directive in my own CPU. While completing this book, she would bring food in a way that made me feel like *Thoughtrave* was being catered by Craft Services. I am also grateful for my cousin Frank and godmother Mary Vender as well as Christine and Donald Vender and their families.

Thank you again and again goes to my New England Family: The Darts, Obie and Meredith (Oriannah and Mariellah), Joliannah and John (Johannah and Hadley), Sarah and Matt Jasinski, Matthew Benton, Jan and Martin Benton. Special thanks to our extended family, especially Amy Richardson and Molly McKee.

Always in our corner: Sam, Tracey, Maddie, and Alex Fritch. More beach time please. Less laptop and phone time. More. Water. And. Sand. Please.

Eric Hardekopf has been my BFF since high school. You know you have a friend for life when you can show up with nothing – absolutely nothing – and no place to go like we did August 2015 and have him respond: "So, you're fucked. Come on in. (beat) Beer?" Tina, Tatum, and Delaney are his rock star family and I cannot thank them enough for being great cousins and amazing people always but especially during our time of terrifying uncertainty.

Dennis Moritz and Laurie Carlos are lifelong friends whose work inspired so much of my early studies and writing I wouldn't even know how to unhook the three of us. Instead, we beat on. It is my great hope and pleasure to make our gatherings weekly and our work constant, any medium, anytime. I very much love you both.

Jill Thompsett entered my life when I was quite convinced that I, not a project, was going to die. A few months after my father passed in 1984, I met her. We've been verbally abusing each other ever since. In August and September 2012, when I wanted to make a run for music producer and composer, I could hear the sigh of relief and immediate encouragement in her emails and Facebook messages as well as our phone conversations. "Bobby Baum is back." Thank you for being a royal pain in the ass and for loving someone like me who probably should have been hospitalized for being an equal if not more intense pain in the ass. Yes. You love me. So. Stop. Special thanks to her kids, Jake and Jenna, for welcoming their uncle, aunt, and cousins into their lives in August 2015 and beyond. Also, special thanks to her mom Candy and her father Lloyd: thank you for Jill and for always being there for me. The hospitality and love shown by Jill's siblings (and kids) are legion: Jen, Aaron, Ryanne and Jaci; Scott, Julie, Jack, Lily and Luke; and Danielle, John, Riley, and Carter.

George, Theo, Eli, and Ollie are my most honorable sons, the fight club Stefani referred to as the "Ministers of Ministry" the night she invited us to join her Haus of Gaga by way of creating images that included her emblem. Thank you for believing in all we have been doing probably as long as you can remember. They inspire me daily as well as keep each other entertained during the long hours and days and weeks and months their father works overtime to change the game for their children. I do, however, regret not replacing the Xbox. I sure do miss those long wait times playing *Call of Duty*, especially the Zombie DLCs. (It's probably time for us to detox from all the soda we drank across the last eighteen months especially…)

All Michelle Mielewski Baum, my wife, wanted was a normal life and family. Sorry. That was never going to happen. (With a nod to Adam Ferrara for paraphrasing his joke.) We've suffered many nights, days, weeks, months, years of anxiety trying to stay employed, attempting to give our kids the best of all possible lives under the worst of all possible economic conditions: the downsizing of everything (see the novel Michelle inspired called *Smile*). From those fated moments at CatholicU in 1990 and again in 1992 to this moment, I cannot thank her enough for loving me… someone who always feels quite alien in this world but never when seen through her eyes. She has been and remains my home away from home. I will love her forever.

Finally, for David Bowie. The early morning of his death announcement my spiritual systems experienced a brown out. I needed to restart everything. It was the strangest 3:30–7:30 a.m. of my life. Every project. Every draft. Everything coming to completion. Old collaborators. New collaborations. Education projects. Everything came online again as if hacked, as if upgraded and restored. Everything that transpired in January and February 2016 was a result of this strange black star event. I know it. Let's dance.

Robert Craig Baum is the author of Itself *(Atropos Press, 2011) which Avital Ronell described as "a dense, difficult, and feisty takedown of key philosophical concepts that define our modernity and beleaguer ethical certitudes." Baum received his BA in Philosophy from The Catholic University of America, MALS from Dartmouth College, and PhD from the European Graduate School. He is a professor, administrator, playwright, composer, producer, and a board member of the Main Street Museum. His upcoming works of mourning include* The One to Come *(Heidegger, National Socialism, and* existenz-philosophie*), What Remains (a philosophical memoir disclosing the "life gives" or* Ereignis *potentiality of suicide),* A Naughty Night to Swim In *(fifteen short memoirs narrating/medicating battles with madness), and* Smile *(a slipstream novel combining his love of Clive Barker, Annie Dillard, C.S. Lewis, Herman Melville, and Kurt Vonnegut). He lives in New York with his wife and four boys.*

Brianne Bolin is a professor and a co-founder of PrecariCorps (with Joe Fruscione and Kat Jacobsen), an independent nonprofit organization offering much-needed financial, emotional, and professional support to adjunct faculty. She received her BA and MA in English from Eastern Illinois University, a state school whose existence is threatened at the time of publication by the Illinois government's refusal to pass a budget (#FundEIU). She is the co-creator of the television show CAMPU$ *(a Kubrickian exploration of corporate college life).*

George Elerick is a professor at the Global Center for Advanced Studies, a digital and terrestrial education movement that seeks to offer free higher education to all worldwide. He is also a human rights activist who uses filmmaking, acting, philosophy, spirituality and journalism as keys to creating a ethical and political space of self and community inquiry. Elerick is the founder of the Anti-Racism Coalition in the UK as well as a performer, writer, filmmaker, and co-producer at N1Productions.

Lady Gaga is a Grammy® Award winning musician, television and film star, and global philanthropist (Born This Way Foundation). Her albums include The Fame *(2008),* The Fame Monster *(2009),* Born This Way *(2011),* Artpop *(2013), and* Cheek to Cheek *(2014). As of this printing she has received over two hundred awards for her work and stars in* American Horror Story: Hotel.

"I remember my father; I remember everything."

– Central Station (1998)